EVERYDAY Comforts

Ideas for Making Your Home a Haven

Better Homes and Gardens® Books
Des Moines, Iowa

Better Homes and Gardens® Books
An imprint of Meredith® Books

Everyday Comforts
Editor: Vicki L. Ingham
Art Director: Sundie Ruppert
Copy Chief: Terri Fredrickson
Copy and Production Editor: Victoria Forlini
Editorial Operations Manager: Karen Schirm
Managers, Book Production: Pam Kvitne, Marjorie J. Schenkelberg
Contributing Copy Editor: Jane Woychick
Contributing Proofreaders: Beth Lastine, Kenya McCullum, Susan Sanfrey
Indexer: Sharon Duffy
Illustrations: Lori Gould
Electronic Production Coordinator: Paula Forest
Editorial and Design Assistants: Kaye Chabot, Karen McFadden, Mary Lee Gavin

Meredith® Books
Publisher and Editor in Chief: James D. Blume
Design Director: Matt Strelecki
Managing Editor: Gregory H. Kayko
Executive Editor, Home Decorating and Design: Denise L. Caringer

Director, Operations: George A. Susral
Director, Production: Douglas M. Johnston

Vice President and General Manager: Douglas J. Guendel

Better Homes and Gardens® Magazine
Editor in Chief: Karol DeWulf Nickell

Meredith Publishing Group
President, Publishing Group: Stephen M. Lacy
Vice President-Publishing Director: Bob Mate

Meredith Corporation
Chairman and Chief Executive Officer: William T. Kerr

Chairman of the Executive Committee: E. T. Meredith III

All of us at Better Homes and Gardens® Books are dedicated to providing you with information and ideas to enhance your home. We welcome your comments and suggestions. Write to us at: Better Homes and Gardens Books, Home Decorating and Design Editorial Department, 1716 Locust St., Des Moines, IA 50309-3023.

If you would like to purchase any of our home decorating and design, cooking, crafts, gardening, or home improvement books, check wherever quality books are sold. Or visit us at: bhgbooks.com

Cover Photograph: Kim Cornelison

EVERYDAY Comforts

The dictionary defines comfort as a feeling of encouragement or contentment, a satisfying or enjoyable experience, and consolation in times of trouble or anxiety. "Comfortable" is the word most people choose to describe the way they want their homes to be, and that description refers to more than the merely physical aspect of comfort. Home is the harbor you set out from and the haven you return to. Decorating might seem to be more about surface than spirit, but in fact, the setting you create has a big impact on whether rooms embrace and nurture you or keep you at arm's length. The choices you make—how you dress the windows to maximize light, how you arrange furniture to foster relaxation, and how you display collections and objects to please the eye and kindle memories—help define your home as a place that restores and rejuvenates those who live there.

It's no surprise that the quest for comfort arises as a response to the ever-accelerating pace and stresses of modern life. Managing the stress without imploding requires making choices about your time and resources. One of the keys to finding respite is mindfulness—being in the moment, paying attention to those things that bring you joy, and making the time to appreciate them. Whatever delights you—patterns of light and shadow, the smell of wet earth in spring, the laughter of children—take a moment to acknowledge it and appreciate it. It doesn't have to be a lot of time—30 seconds to drink in a cloudless blue sky, 20 minutes to read in bed. Everyday comforts are those ordinary pleasures and little luxuries with which you bless yourself and others. Simply by noticing, affirming, and receiving them, you lift these gifts above the commonplace and embrace their power to nurture and heal.

Although each of us has a different concept of what constitutes comfort, I hope the ideas in this book will help you identify your own sources of joy. (For even more inspiration, visit our website, bhg.com/bhgrelax.) As you find ways to incorporate these ideas into your decorating, you'll discover an added dimension of satisfaction in the process of making your home a welcoming place to be.

Vicki Ingham

Vicki Ingham,
Editor

light

8 BASK... in the sun and use light to sculpt space, creating a welcoming, nurturing atmosphere in your home.

fragrance

30 INHALE... deeply and draw on the power of fragrance to evoke memories, to relieve stress, or simply to treat yourself to the pleasure of wonderful scents.

sound

42 LISTEN... carefully to filter out the noise of life and focus on the sounds that bring you joy.

bed
dream

52 DREAM... sweet dreams in a bedroom that's a sanctuary, a place of comfort and security that restores you physically and emotionally.

bath

66 RELAX... in a bubble bath or under the stream of a hot shower. Your bathroom can become an at-home spa.

spaces

storage

flowers

focal points

tabletop

nourishing the
Senses

light

Morning sunlight streaming through windows sings a wake-up call, urging you to be up and about, rejoicing in the day. Afternoon light, with its warm and lazy rays, beckons you to stretch out like a cat and take a nap. As the sun sets, it paints your walls copper and gold with rich radiance that sends a subliminal message to relax and unwind. Whether it comes from the sun, lamps, or candles, light sculpts space and creates a welcoming, nurturing atmosphere. Decorating with light involves thoughtful use of both natural illumination and artificial lighting. The right amount and type of light for each purpose—reading, cooking, working, entertaining—makes rooms comforting and comfortable.

follow the sun

Each day the path of sunlight into your home changes as the sun makes its seasonal trek north or south of the equator. Give yourself time to enjoy the patterns of light that fall on furnishings, which become natural still lifes painted by a sunbeam. The solar artistry is transitory, but the minutes you take to absorb and appreciate it can have an uplifting impact on your mood.

Leave windows scantily clad to let in the maximum amount of light. Roller blinds that fit into the window frame provide privacy at night without covering up handsome architecture.

▲ For an unexpected window dressing, showcase a vintage frock. Choose a north-facing window, because strong sunlight will cause the fabric to deteriorate.

◄ Scrim, a coarsely woven cloth available in fabric stores and theatrical-supply shops, drapes gracefully across a window, screening an unattractive view without blocking the light.

▶ Simple sheers gathered on a tension rod or wall-mounted pole softly filter sunlight.

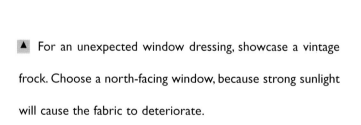

When you position furniture, consider where the sunlight falls during the times you're most likely to use the room. To bask in the light at breakfast, you might need to move the table a little closer to the windows rather than centering it under the chandelier.

Showcase a collection of colored glass jars and vases on your windowsill. When the sun strikes

the glass, beams of blue (or green, yellow, or red, depending on your glass) will play across the

walls. You can also color the light entering the room by propping a vintage stained-glass window

on the sill or suspending it from eye hooks in the window frame. Remember, however, that when

the sun isn't striking the window directly, the stained glass dims the light coming through and may

make the room feel darker.

A house that glows with lamplight at dusk sends out a friendly welcome. Give yourself a cheerful homecoming by putting lamps on timers set to go on at dusk. For porch lights, use photoelectric sensors that screw into the fixture; the light will come on automatically at dusk and remain on until dawn, offering security as well as comfort. For the ultimate in lighting control, install a wireless remote-control system that lets you turn the lights in your home on and off from your car (for more information, see page 186).

let it glow

Candlelight banishes darkness and evokes meditation and relaxation. To diffuse the gentle light still further, place the candle and its holder inside a gauzy sack of sheer organza, *right*. (For simple sewing instructions, turn to page 172.)

Candle sconces, *opposite*, offer an easy alternative to electric sconces, washing the wall with a cozy glow. Make a wire harness for a jelly-jar candle and suspend it from a reproduction or vintage iron bracket to warm a hallway or dining room wall (instructions are on page 172).

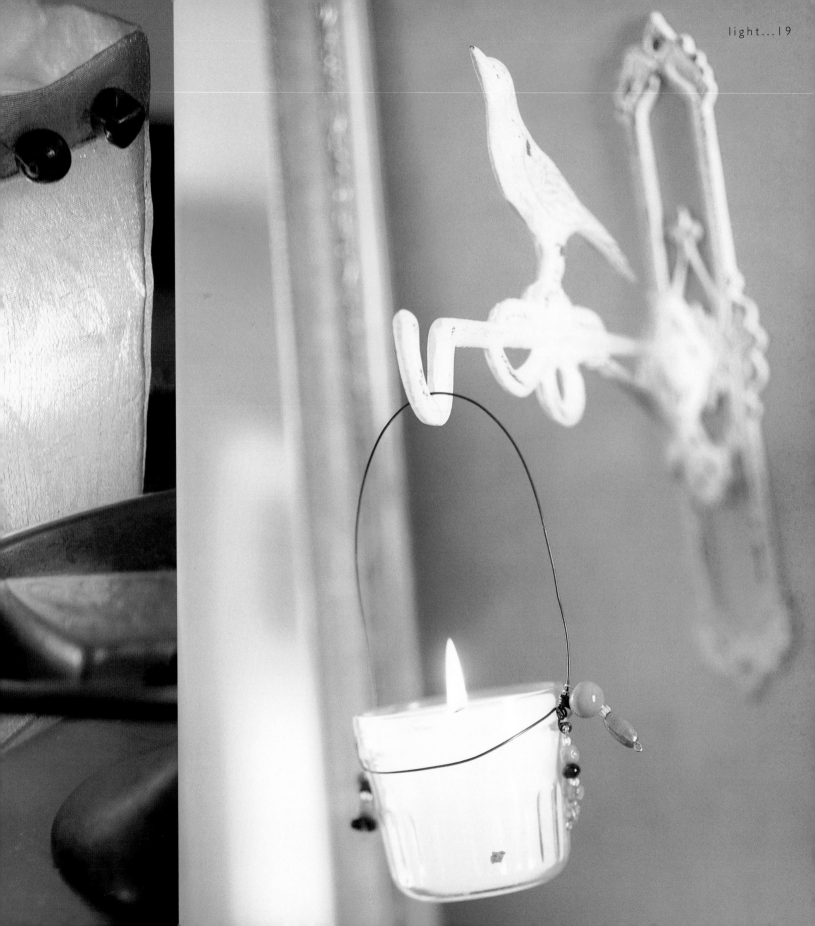

create drama

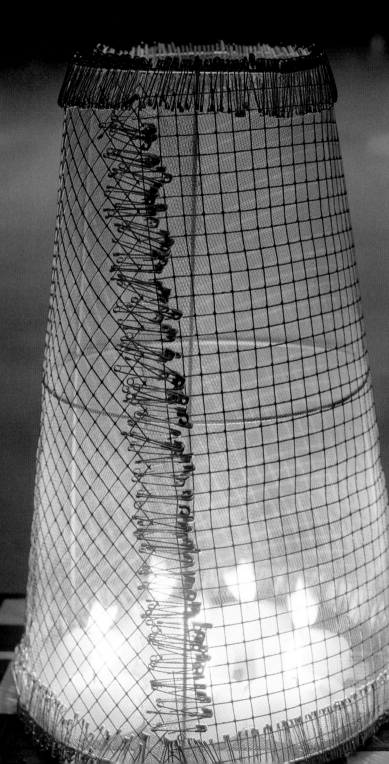

Citronella candles perform the practical function of discouraging mosquitoes while illuminating your patio party. To create a mood of casual relaxation, however, supplement these workhorses with tapers, pillars, and votive candles that supply an air of beauty and romance. Placed along paths, around the garden, at poolside, and on tables, candles twinkle with a festive glow and shed a surprising amount of light. Enhance their decorative impact with shades made from tomato cages or topiary forms. The mesh shade, *left,* is made by wrapping a tomato cage with hardware cloth and fine-mesh window screen, secured decoratively with safety pins. (For instructions, see page 173.)

▼ Candleholders suspended from metal brackets can be mounted on fence posts or railings to illuminate a deck or garden border. Look for candleholders and brackets like the one *below* in garden-supply catalogs or garden centers.

▲ Cluster candles on trays for greater impact. To protect the flames from breezes, use votive holders that are taller than the tea lights or candles. Or stand pillar candles inside canning jars or hurricane lamps to protect the flames. "Lampshades" made from topiary forms and vellum amplify the candlelight (see page 172 for instructions).

1   Fashion your own candle sconce using supplies from the crafts store and hardware store

(see page 173 for instructions and a materials list). Hang a pair over the mantel or on a wall where

no one will inadvertently brush against them.   2   For a quick summertime table decoration,

stand a pillar candle in a metal bucket filled with sand.

Evoke romance

Dining by candlelight puts guests at ease and promotes a convivial mood. A vintage chandelier outfitted with tapers brings an air of old-world elegance to the room by day; at night, the flickering light evokes mystery and romance. Shop flea markets and antiques shops for old chandeliers that have not yet been electrified. Reproduction versions with electric candles will be easier to find; low-watt bulbs and a dimmer switch let you capture the mood of candlelight without the potential mess of dripping wax.

add sparkle

Instead of the usual ceiling light in a

bathroom or powder room, install a

chandelier. It's unexpected—you usually

find chandeliers in dining rooms and

entries—so it lifts the room out of the

ordinary with a fillip of luxury. You can

have an old candle chandelier

electrified for you by a lamp and lighting

store. Hang it to one side of the vanity

mirror, rather than centering it in the

room, for a casually elegant effect.

Amplify natural light by positioning oversize mirrors strategically. Mount large mirrors

on wall studs for security. To make the dressing mirror *opposite*, the homeowner

replaced the center panel of a door with mirror and added wrought-iron feet.

use lamplight

Place table lamps around the room to

sculpt space into pools of warm light. For

the greatest versatility, plug lamps into lamp

dimmers, available at hardware stores.

These allow you to ease the light level up

for reading or down for softer ambience.

◄ Give a new look to an old lampshade with a slipcover made from a pleated paper shade. Look for the shades in the window treatment section of home centers and home decorating stores. Cut the shade to size and add your own painted design (see page 174 for instructions).

► A flirty little night-light twinkles in a bedroom or bathroom, providing sufficient illumination to keep you (or guests) from bumping into walls or furniture. Assemble the lamp yourself using easy-to-find supplies from a hardware store and art store (see page 175 for instructions).

fragrance

Follow your nose to create comfort in your home. A room that smells good to you will make you feel good too. That's because one of the fastest routes to the brain's control center for well-being is through the 25,000 odor receptors in the nose. It stands to reason, therefore, that fragrance is a potent ally if you want to make guests feel welcome or your family feel relaxed and content. Personal preferences may lead you to choose florals over more exotic scents such as patchouli or ylang-ylang, but enjoy the ordinary aromas as well: Baking bread, freshly brewed coffee, and clean laundry that has dried in the sun invite you to inhale deeply and immerse yourself in the pleasure of the moment.

natural mood lifters

Savor the piercing fragrance of an orange as you peel it—those essential oils that you're releasing can ease nervous tension and stress.

The yeasty aroma of freshly baked bread makes a gentle alarm clock: Use the delayed timer on your bread machine for a

mouthwatering wake-up call.

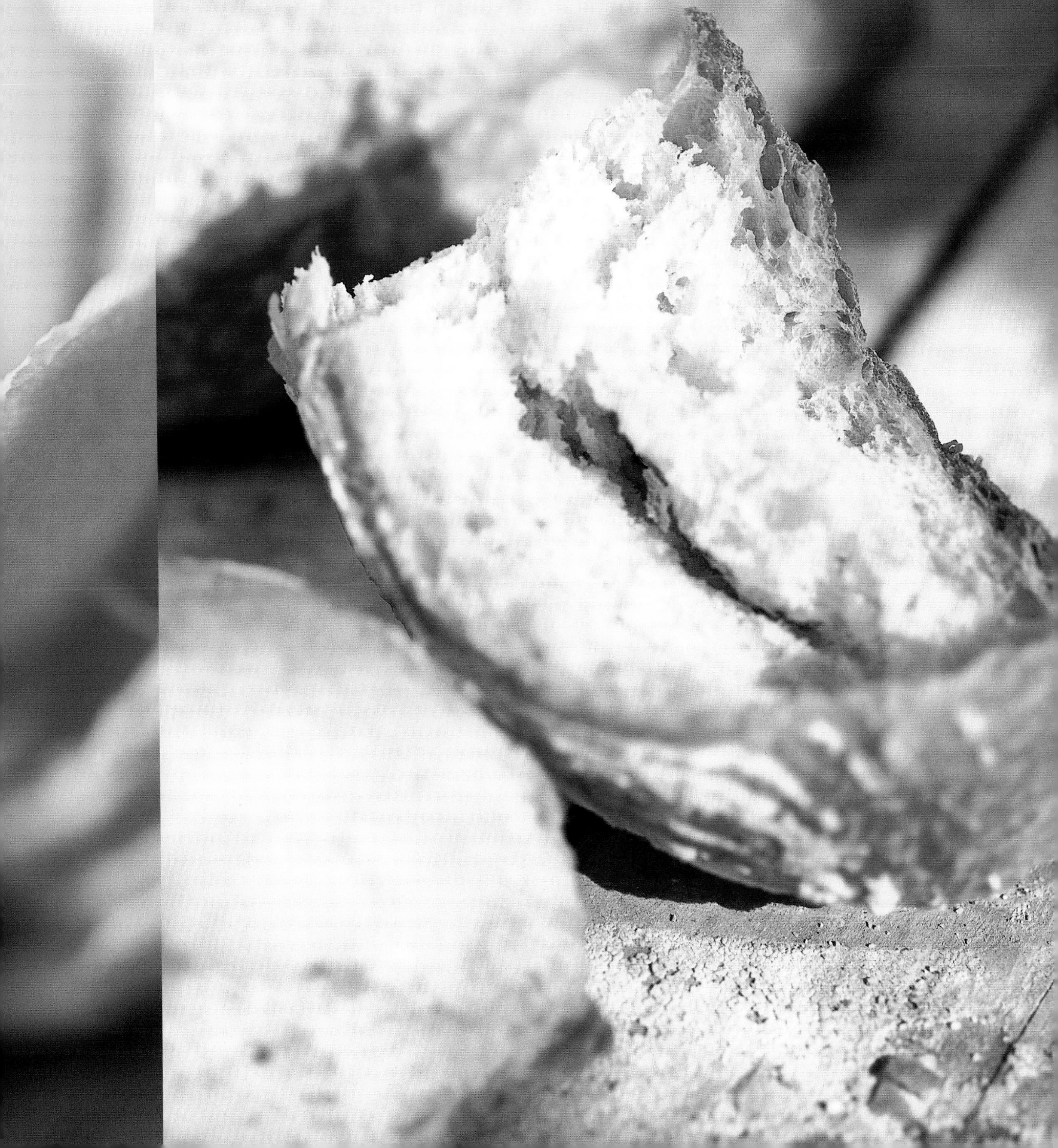

Welcome yourself home with scented geraniums placed by the door, where you can brush the leaves as you pass by, to release the scent. Or hang strongly scented fresh flowers, such as lilacs, on the door or in your entry. Herbs such as rosemary and sage, *above,* stimulate beta waves in the brain, making you feel more alert. So along with your morning coffee, rub some rosemary leaves and inhale the aroma to kick-start your day.

Fragrant flowers from the garden help create a welcoming atmosphere in entry halls, living rooms, and bedrooms. Place them at nose level—on a tall table in the entry, on a coffee table or side table in the living room, and at bedside in the bedroom. Most flowers won't scent a whole room: You have to come close and breathe deeply to experience the pleasure of the smell. Breathing deeply is key to relaxation, so aromatic flowers reward you twice.

lovely lavender

Take a cue from the French and scent your linens and laundry with the fragrance of lavender. Commercially available lavender waters can be added to the rinse water in your washing machine or spritzed onto fabrics before you press them. You can also make your own lavender spray by mixing alcohol-based lavender-scented toilet water with distilled water.

Eau de linge
à la Lavande
n Lavande

▲ Because lavender is said to encourage relaxation and induce sleep, it's perfect for filling a sachet to tuck under your pillow.

◄ Lavender's clean, fresh scent commends it for closets too. Keep clothes smelling sweet with individual sachets slipped over the hanger.

► Add lavender buds to a purchased buckwheat-hull pillow to ensure a good night's rest. Buckwheat-hull pillows, which are widely available at home decorating stores and variety stores, conform to the shape of your head and neck, providing support where you need it. (For instructions on how to make these sachets and pillows, see pages 174–175.)

indulge...

Aromatherapy is an alternative form of healing that uses essential oils extracted from plants. Most scented candles, bath oils, bath fizzies, and body lotions are made with synthetic oils, which won't provide the medical benefits claimed for true aromatherapy; but these products can lift your spirits simply because you like the smell, so go ahead and enjoy. Bath fizzies, *top left,* release their fragrance when you drop them into the bath water. Lemon juice and sea salts, *top right*, make for an invigorating soak.

sound

Most people are so accustomed to a constant undercurrent of noise that true silence is disconcerting. The antidote to stress-inducing noise isn't necessarily silence, however. Music "soothes the savage beast" and speaks directly to the heart. Of course, one person's music is another person's audio irritant, so music must be used thoughtfully in shaping the atmosphere of a home. Sounds of nature are music too: Birds singing, crickets chirping, the wind in the leaves, waves on the shore—all of these bring joy and a sense of peace if you take the time to stop and listen. The murmuring conversation of burbling water is so effective as a stress reducer that it has been tamed and channeled into fountains, indoors and out.

water music

An outdoor fountain requires nothing more than a container and a pump (and a nearby source of electricity), but your embellishments can turn it into a focal point. Here, an antique millstone rests on a bed of river rocks that conceal a 5-foot-diameter plastic tub holding the pump and water (see page 176 for details). Sinking the tub into the ground creates the illusion of a spring-fed pool. If you wish to make a feature of the container itself, show it off above ground and surround it with plants and statuary. To bring natural-looking waterfalls and pools into your garden (without the aid of a real creek), talk to a landscape architect who specializes in water features.

Plan for satisfying sounds throughout the house. In a home office, please both eye and ear with an indoor fountain that's a work of art. For the bedroom, look for a small CD player that fits comfortably on a nightstand or dresser.

laugh often

and listen to nature

feathering your

Nest

the bed

The bedroom is a sanctuary; it's also one of the most enjoyable rooms to decorate

with an eye to everyday pleasures. You can lavish attention on the little luxuries

here: soft clean sheets, pretty pillows, and a plump duvet; a dressing table with your

favorite lotions or perfumes; a collection of photos to bring to mind family and

friends. It's a place to take time for the nighttime rituals that bring the day to a close

with comfortable familiarity. In this, your private domain, the bed is the throne,

your place to curl up (with or without the kids and the cat) and be restored.

Outfitted with a nearby table for a lamp, books, and other necessities, the bed may

also be your reading room, your meditation space, or your personal retreat.

create a cocoon

Canopies and curtains wrap the bed with a sense of snug enclosure. Use whisper-sheer fabrics to envelop the bed with delicious luxury. If you have a four-poster bed with top rails, tie on tab-style curtains. If your bed has no canopy structure, create a curtained effect by attaching columns of fabric to the ceiling overhead (see page 176 for instructions) or by layering scarves over monofilament hung from the ceiling (see page 62).

A headboard and stacks of pillows provide back support for

reading in bed. Faux suede covers this headboard, which is outlined

with upholstery tacks. Wool curtains hang from antique polo mallets, and

stacked luggage serves as bedside table and blanket chest.

collect vintage linens

Although vintage sheets are rare, pillowcases can still be found at antiques shops and estate sales and through online sources (see page 188). If old cotton or linen cases are in good condition, allow yourself the luxury of the soft fabric against your skin and put the cases to use. Cotton pillowcases, including those with embroidered edges, may be machine washed on the gentle cycle. Iron them before putting them on the bed, so they'll look crisp and fresh. Launder linen cases by soaking them in a commercial linen wash; then line-dry and press them.

► For a cozy, cottage-style look, shop for tablecloths and draperies from the first half of the 20th century and use them to make duvet covers and bed skirts. Even stained or damaged cloths can be cut up and stitched into pillows or cafe curtains and valances. Pairs of old draperies look too heavy by today's standards, but you can drape one panel over each window like a swag or scarf.

◄ Turn an embroidered dresser scarf from the 1950s into a handy bed caddy. To make it, fold the scarf in half, right sides facing and short ends matching. Fold one short end back to form a cuff (both embroidered ends will be faceup). Stitch the sides close to the edges. Then make two lines of stitching for pockets. Tuck the remaining end of the dresser scarf under the mattress, securing it with mattress pins (look for these at fabric stores).

Add the romance of a fireplace to your bedroom without remodeling. All you need is an electric receptacle and about 4 feet of wall space to accommodate the firebox insert and cabinet of an electric fireplace. Realistic holographic flames flicker above faux logs, and the unit produces forced-air heat, which you can turn off to enjoy the fireplace in warm weather (see page 188 for more information).

cozy up

▲ The ideal setting for reading in bed includes a firm headboard you can

lean against, plump pillows to support your back, and wall-mounted read-

ing lamps on swivel arms, so you can position the light where you need it.

Look for these swivel-arm lamps at home improvement centers. They

screw into the wall, and the cords plug into the nearest receptacle.

Instant canopy

Turn a plain bed into a romantic focal point with a canopy stitched from chiffon and sheer scarves. Collect the scarves from flea markets, thrift shops, and your own dresser. Choose scarves of a similar weight and with some common colors, and add panels of solid chiffon to provide a visual link (and a relief from all the pattern). Clear monofilament stitched to the canopy and tied through screw eyes suspends the fabric over the bed. (For detailed instructions, see page 177.)

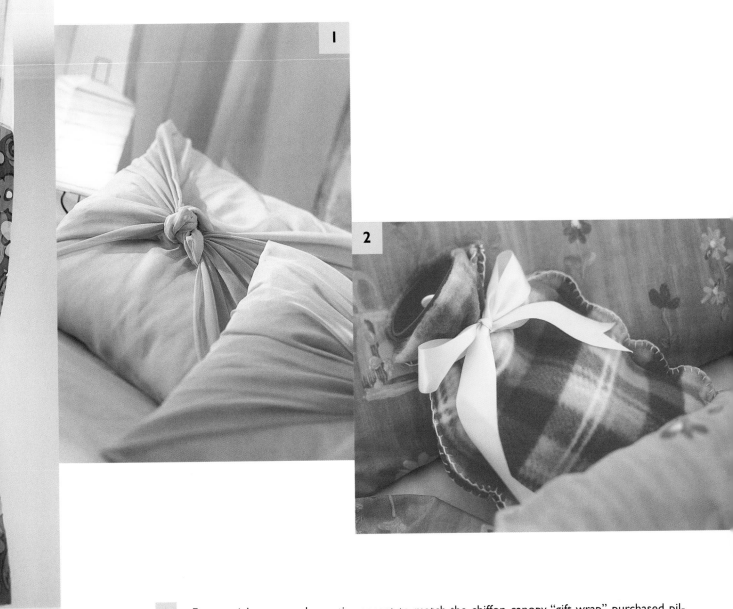

1　For a quick, no-sew decorating accent to match the chiffon canopy, "gift-wrap" purchased pillows in chiffon, knotting the ends on the front of the pillow.　2　Warming blankets make the bed toasty, but for old-fashioned comfort, snuggle under the covers with a fleece-covered hot water bottle (see page 177 for sewing instructions). Wrapped in cheerful fuzzy fabric, the hot water bottle is also nice for children to cuddle with when they're not feeling well.

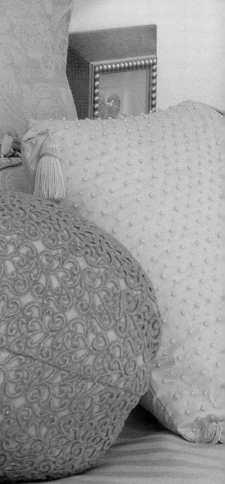

▲ Even a modest-sized bedroom can feel like a master suite retreat if you bring in a chair for reading, an ottoman for your feet, and a table or two to hold books and necessities. If you have the space beside the bed, use a long side table instead of the usual nightstand. It offers more storage and display space and creates a comfortable, mix-don't-match look. Soften hard edges with fabric: Drape a shawl over the bedside table, for example, and slipcover the headboard and footboard for a look of well-padded comfort.

On the table beside your bed, group meaningful objects and photos of family and friends. They'll be the last things you see at night and the first you see on waking. A bedside lamp that's tall enough for reading in bed sheds warm light on the arrangement. (A three-way lamp or a lamp dimmer lets you turn the wattage up for reading or down for a moody glow.) Hang a small piece of artwork right next to the bed, lower than you would ordinarily place a framed piece. The effect is intimate—a little visual treat.

the bath

A long soak in a tub of hot water is one of the top five ways that more than half the Moms in America relax. Hot tubs and spas with precision-focused jets of water can massage aching muscles and joints and encourage deep relaxation, but you can shed the stresses of the day in an ordinary bathtub too. The first step is to give yourself the time, even if it's only 15 minutes. A spa pillow that attaches to the tub with suction cups comfortably supports your neck, and a tub caddy can hold a book or magazine so you can read. If you're a shower person, the perfect water massage is only a showerhead away. New designs offer luxurious style as well as a fabulous shower, and most you can install yourself. See page 189 for more information.

pamper yourself

Lift the daily bath or shower out of humdrum routine with little luxuries. Candlelight quiets the mind and scents the bathroom with calming fragrance. Choose jasmine, rose, chamomile, or lavender to promote relaxation. Keep fluffy cotton towels handy in rustproof metal baskets for a look that's light and airy. A terry cloth-covered dressing stool is practical and fun—or make your own terry slipcover for a small chair (see page 73).

mmmmm ...

Step out of the shower and into a toasty towel that's been warming on a heated towel rack. Choose either a freestanding or a wall-mounted model; most simply plug into an electric receptacle (see page 189 for information). Other affordable luxuries include lavender sachets to scent your towels, a rolling-pin-style foot massager, and a bookrack tub caddy.

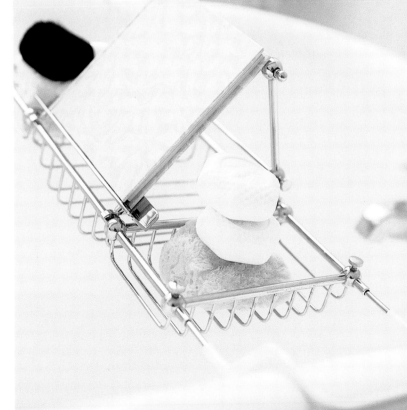

Give yourself a comfy place to sit and dry your toes. Terry cloth makes an unexpected and wonderfully tactile slipcover for a wooden folding chair. The skirted seat cushion and tie-on top are sewn from bath towels (for instructions, see page 178). To cover a more conventional chair, buy terry cloth by the yard. Unwind with a spa pillow and towels embroidered with encouraging words, such as "relax" or "soak" (for instructions, see page 179). Look in the Yellow Pages under "Monograms" to find a company that will stitch the words onto your towels.

... ooohhh

A foot soak restores your feet—and your mood. A portable foot massager works its magic with bubbling water, but a small tub of warm (not hot) water works too. Soaks and massages soothe tired feet by promoting better blood circulation. Pat your "piggies" dry and rub on a cooling foot gel to reinvigorate your feet.

Be kind to your hands with a home paraffin wax treatment. It's a classic spa experience that softens skin and eases achy joints. The paraffin melts inside a thermostatically controlled container; you dip your hands (or elbows or feet) repeatedly into the wax, for as many as 15 layers. When the wax cools, peel it off and massage the emollients into your skin.

If you love showers, there's nothing worse than a weak, wimpy spray—and nothing better than a good, firm stream massaging your head and neck and wrapping you in a cloak of warm water. If your home has low water pressure, compare showerheads and choose the one that delivers the most water under those conditions. Low-flow showerheads (which consume no more than 2.5 gallons per minute) save water and money, but since the mid-1990s, even standard showerheads use no more than 5.5 gallons per minute.

... aaahhh

spaces

The stress of living by the calendar and the clock can leave you breathless from rushing to meet one appointment or deadline after another. The remedy requires an act of will: Give yourself the gift of a few minutes to step off the treadmill without guilt. Establishing comfort zones indoors and out can help you unwind. The zone may be as simple as a comfortable chair in a quiet corner, a rocking chair on the porch, or a hammock in the backyard. For family spaces, arrange furniture to create a room within a room where you can play or relax together. Choose furnishings that encourage you to be at ease: chairs and sofas that embrace you, places to put your feet up, lamps for ambience and the game or book at hand.

curl up

Create a nesting spot that's as welcoming as your grandmother's lap—a safe, cushiony place to curl up and dream. An upholstered chair is a must, a chair-and-a-half is perfect. Keep a quilt or throw handy for snuggling under on chilly afternoons. Angling the dresser across a corner can give the room a greater feeling of depth and open up space for the chair. Use color to create serenity: Shades of white, cream, butter yellow, and beige envelop the bedroom in a relaxed, airy atmosphere.

Encourage yourself to relax by setting the stage with sink-back seating, a place to put your feet, and a good reading lamp (an adjustable one is ideal). You also need a place to put your stuff: A filing cabinet can double as a side table and magazine storage box; a coffee table lets you keep favorite books in plain sight.

relax with a book

use pill

Plump pillows make even the cushiest sofa look more inviting. Use them to add color accents in a neutral room or to emphasize one color over another in your room scheme. For a seasonal accent, change the pillow covers.

◀ A patchwork of corduroy in plum and pink suggests winter warmth.

▼ A printed sheer is light and summery and simply wraps over your existing pillow. Both covers are easy to make—see page 179 for instructions.

power

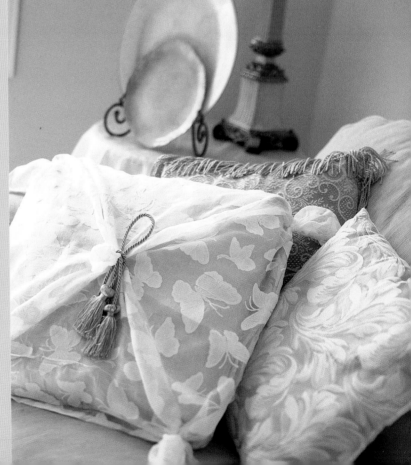

Comfort zones are the places you're drawn to for reading, dreaming, or relaxing with family and friends. What's the secret to carving out a comfort zone? Start with sofas and chairs that have generously rounded shapes covered in casual, easy-care fabrics. Add pillows to tuck behind your back or beside you, and provide each seat with a convenient surface for a cup of tea, a snack, some books, or needlework. If you usually eat on the run, make a point of slowing down and having a meal in your comfort zone. Even if you opt for carryout, the experience feels more special when you're sitting on pillows in front of the fire.

In good weather, comfort zones edge closer to the outdoors or move outside altogether. Position a settee to take advantage of breezes through an open door or window. Furnish a screen porch as you would a room inside—hang a chandelier with votive candles over the table and soften the wire-mesh "walls" with gauzy curtains made of theatrical scrim, mosquito netting, or inexpensive cotton sheeting. Heavy eye screws hold curtain cable taut between the posts, and curtain clips catch up the fabric. Buy mosquito netting by the yard online or check home decorating stores. Look for curtain cable and curtain clips at fabric stores or order through catalogs—see page 186 for sources. When the curtains become dusty, unclip them and put them in the washing machine.

When life was slower, the front porch was where people rested in the afternoon or gathered after supper to exchange news or tell stories. Layering the porch floor with a weather-resistant rug defines a roomlike feeling, and rocking chairs invite relaxing. Secret gardens offer another kind of relaxation, *opposite*. With walls of lattice and greenery, fountains, and found sculpture, a garden room off the back or side of your house can become a spiritual and physical retreat.

make time to daydream

Some people find their spirits revived in interaction; others, in drawing apart. Whether you prefer the friendly sociability of the porch or deck or the quiet seclusion of an enclosed garden, lay claim to some piece of nature as your comfort zone. You may not have time to sit and rock on the porch or snooze away the afternoon in a hammock, but take a minute to stop and focus: Feel the breeze on your skin; smell the newly cut grass; listen to the wildly joyous song of a mockingbird. These simple pleasures are free for the taking and can restore the spirit.

stay cool

Stacks of cheerful terry cloth pillows
make poolside lounging more
comfortable. Use one bath towel for
each 20x20-inch pillow. To prevent
raveling, zigzag-stitch or serge the raw
edges after cutting. Stitch jumbo
rickrack into the seams and sew an
invisible zipper into one edge to make
laundering easy.

storage

Perhaps you love to surround yourself with collectibles and memorabilia. Or perhaps the abundance of stuff that once felt cozy now feels claustrophobic and you're up for a massive decluttering campaign. In either case, creative storage solutions can help you achieve serenity through order. Organizing the things you need and the things you love, putting some away and showcasing others, lets you banish the chaos of clutter and bring a sense of calm to your rooms. Unconventional or repurposed storage options, such as picnic tins used as towel holders or old toolboxes as mudroom catchalls, go beyond the merely functional to add style and character to your home.

home work

In a home office, utilitarian shelving offers more storage surface than a conventional bookcase. Baskets and boxes hold paperwork and supplies and make good use of the deep between-shelf space. For rustic charm, hang old fruit crates on the wall *(opposite)* to serve as shelves. Sand the rough interior of each crate to remove splinters, then mount the crates on studs for security.

1 Why buy plastic desk accessories when repurposed items can do the job and add character too?

An old muffin tin organizes pushpins, rubber bands, paper clips, and other small necessities. 2 A

slightly rusty wrought-iron garden cart comes indoors to serve as a television stand. The bottom shelf

holds the VCR and videocassettes and is high enough to accommodate a basket of magazines below.

Corner office

Any corner can become a center for
homework or office tasks with a build-
it-yourself cupboard and a desk angled
below. Shuttered doors let you hide
clutter. To build the corner unit, start
with a pair of window shutters from a
home center and plan to hinge each
one to a 2-inch trim piece. The shutter
dimensions will determine the height
and width of the cupboard, which you
build from ¾-inch plywood (see page
180 for instructions). Alternatively,
check antiques stores and flea
markets for old wall-hung corner
cupboards that you can adapt to the
same purpose.

tidy up...

◄ Creative storage can be a form of display. Chenille throws or fleece lap blankets rolled up and laid in an antique dough bowl are handy for cuddling while watching television. And they add a touch of color and texture when they're not in use.

▼ If you know you'll never get all those snapshots filed in photo albums, pile them in a big silver punch bowl instead. Keep the bowl close to the sofa so you can enjoy the photos whenever the mood strikes.

▲ An old toolbox or trunk positioned beside the door gives kids a place to drop their backpacks when they come home from school—and your entry will still look neat and orderly. Mount pegs on the wall to organize coats and jackets and, if you have the space, add a bench to sit on while pulling on boots.

store more with style

Use a wooden tool carrier (right) to bring order to the kitchen counter. Brush a coat of paint onto the wood for an easy-to-clean surface. Fill the carrier with cooking staples, platters, and utensils. Slots that might have held screwdrivers can safely store knives. Make the most of shelf storage (opposite) by organizing linens, utensils, even spices in matching wicker baskets. Label the baskets with manila tags from an office supply store. Apply a watercolor wash to the tags for a touch of soft color.

out of sight...

▲ Why waste all that good storage space under the bed? Out-of-season clothes, extra bed linens, and holiday gift wrap can

be tucked out of sight in plywood boxes on wheels. Buy them or make your own (see pages 180–181 for complete instruc-

tions). Handles allow you to pull out the storage units when you need them. Bin-style labels let you identify the contents of the

box at a glance. Cardboard or plastic bins also make good underbed storage units, but they lack the advantage of wheels.

▶ Vintage hatboxes provide stackable storage for individual sweaters; small items such as mittens, scarves, and socks; or crafts

supplies and toys. Shop flea markets and antiques shops for old hatboxes, or buy new ones covered in vintage wallpapers—see

page 190 for more information.

1

1 More storage-as-display ideas: Don't hide pretty necklaces and scarves in jewelry boxes or drawers: Loop them over a wooden hanger to keep them handy and untangled. **2** Tin picnic baskets, lithographed with woven-wicker, plaid, or wood-look designs, were popular in the 1940s and 1950s. Still affordable at antiques shops and online auctions, they're perfect for stashing towels and washcloths.

2

3

4

3   Flea market finds and peg rack molding expand a bathroom's storage potential. A small medicine chest, whether vintage

or new, can hold extra cosmetics, bath supplies, and medicines. Hang a small maple-syrup can on the wall to stow extra rolls

of toilet tissue. Peg rack molding installed below the crown molding all the way around the room provides lots of hangers for

towels, bathrobes, and mesh bags full of tub toys. You could also position it lower, like a plate rail. Screw wooden pegs, evenly

spaced, to 2×4s cut to fit your room's dimensions. Paint the units to match the room's trim and bolt them to the wall studs.

4   Take beauty supplies out of their boxes or bags and store them in apothecary jars. They'll look pretty and inviting, and you

can see at a glance when you need to restock.

Shelve it

Why settle for ordinary shelving when something repurposed can add character and charm? A small bench turned upside down and mounted on the wall, *opposite*, is the perfect size for a bathroom shelf. A reproduction towel rod affixed to the bench's top holds hand towels. A wire étagère, perhaps intended for use in a conservatory, keeps bath towels and soaps within easy reach of the tub. Its light, airy good looks underscore the room's garden feeling, and because you can see through it, the piece enhances the sense of spaciousness in the room.

delighting
in the
Details

flowers

Bouquets from the florist are fine for special occasions, but for everyday pleasure, favor yourself with little bouquets. The flowers don't have to be fancy: Whether you gather them from the garden or buy a bunch at the grocery store, choose colors, shapes, and textures you like. Display them in unconventional containers (a sugar bowl instead of a vase) and in unexpected places (on the kitchen windowsill or beside your reading chair) and you'll find they infuse the room with life. Arranging flowers, leaves, fruits, and grasses is fun, like painting in 3-D, but if you're not con-fident of your skills, don't worry—placing a single sculptural stem in each of five or six glass bottles can be as artistically satisfying as composing a massive bouquet.

treat yourself...

A small bouquet beside the bathroom sink lifts morning and evening rituals out of the routine. If you start with a small container, you won't need many flowers, so you might be able to splurge on something unusual, such as green roses and fragrant freesias. Flowers at bedside make getting up more palatable, *opposite*. Choose common florist's flowers, such as carnations and stock, in uncommon colors for a visual surprise.

Bring the outdoors inside with your own

container-grown lawn. Fill a watertight

container with clean potting soil. Buy

wheat berries or barley seed in bulk

from a natural foods store and soak

them in water for up to eight hours.

Then press them into the soil. Keep the

soil barely moist and place the container

in indirect light. Wheat grass and barley

grass grow best when the temperature is

about 65 to 70 degrees.

... be creative

Don't limit yourself to vases when you arrange flowers. Choosing interesting or unusual containers doubles the decorative

impact of the arrangements. Anything that holds water is a candidate—and if it isn't watertight but can hold a glass or plastic

jar, it can still work. The glass pedestals *opposite* originally supported shelves in Depression-era department-store displays.

Teacups, mugs, pitchers, and tea or biscuit tins, *above*, are perfect receptacles for small clusters of garden flowers and berries.

When composing flowers in a teacup, cut the stems a little shorter than the depth of the teacup; if possible, leave some foliage

on the stems so it can rest on the rim of the cup and hold the blossoms aloft. Any arrangement will last longer if you remove

all the leaves below the waterline and change the water daily. Flower food (from a florist) added to the water also helps.

1   Celebrate May Day every day with a bouquet hung on your front door. Slip a plastic container

inside a metal or wicker basket to hold the flowers. Arrange the stems in your hand; then cut the ends

evenly and drop the bouquet into the container.   2   Team up colorful flowers with equally intense

containers. Pinkish-red roses make the blue and green of this antique opaline glass pop.

Easy art

Think you can't arrange flowers? Don't be so sure. Assemble glass bottles in a variety of heights and fill them with water. Place them on your windowsill and drop one to three stems in each bottle. Choose flowers with long, leggy, irregularly shaped stems—ranunculus, pincushion flower, tulips, and cosmos, for example, will trace interesting lines against the windowpanes. Single stems of astilbe and goldenrod will have a fuller, more feathery look.

think color and shape

The joy of flower arranging lies in looking at materials—not only flowers but also leaves, berries, grasses, fruits, and vegetables—in terms of their colors and shapes and letting these lead you to surprising combinations. 1 Here, for example, grapes and porcelain berry vine inspired the play on purples. Drumstick allium, delphinium, and burgundy miniature carnations fill out the bouquet. 2 Tiny tomatoes and raspberries combine with sunflowers and chrysanthemums in a soup tureen. 3 Crabapples and apples provided the starting point for an arrangement of lilies and astilbe. 4 Rusty red hypericum berries and a matching painted metal container inspired a chairside display of pompon mums, roses, and bells of Ireland. Collect materials from your garden and the roadside and fill in as needed with florist's flowers to make arrangements like these.

1

focal points

A focal point is something that arrests your eye. In terms of room arranging, the focal point is usually a major architectural feature around which furnishings are organized. Focal points also form wherever you gather beloved objects—photos of family, souvenirs from travels, or collections that evoke memories, hold meaning, or delight the eye and the mind. Pay attention to how and where you assemble these objects, and turn them into occasions for joy. At the most basic level, collections of beloved objects make you feel happy simply because you enjoy their shapes, colors, and textures. At another level, however, meaningful mementos acquire a sacred quality and inspire gratitude for the relationships and experiences they represent.

display your passions

Practical souvenirs are fun to use and to display. Instead of tucking a tea set into a cabinet until you're ready to entertain, arrange

key pieces in a still life that will evoke memories daily. A themed composition on an entry table, *opposite,* proclaims the owner's

passion for Paris. When you arrange groups of objects, use odd numbers and at least three

different sizes to create a visually intriguing composition.

Your collecting interests may lead you naturally toward a theme, which you can express in the way you display the objects.

Vintage suitcases, recalling a more romantic era of relaxed travel, stack under a table that holds vintage globes and antique

travel boxes. Binoculars complete the theme of exotic adventures in faraway places.

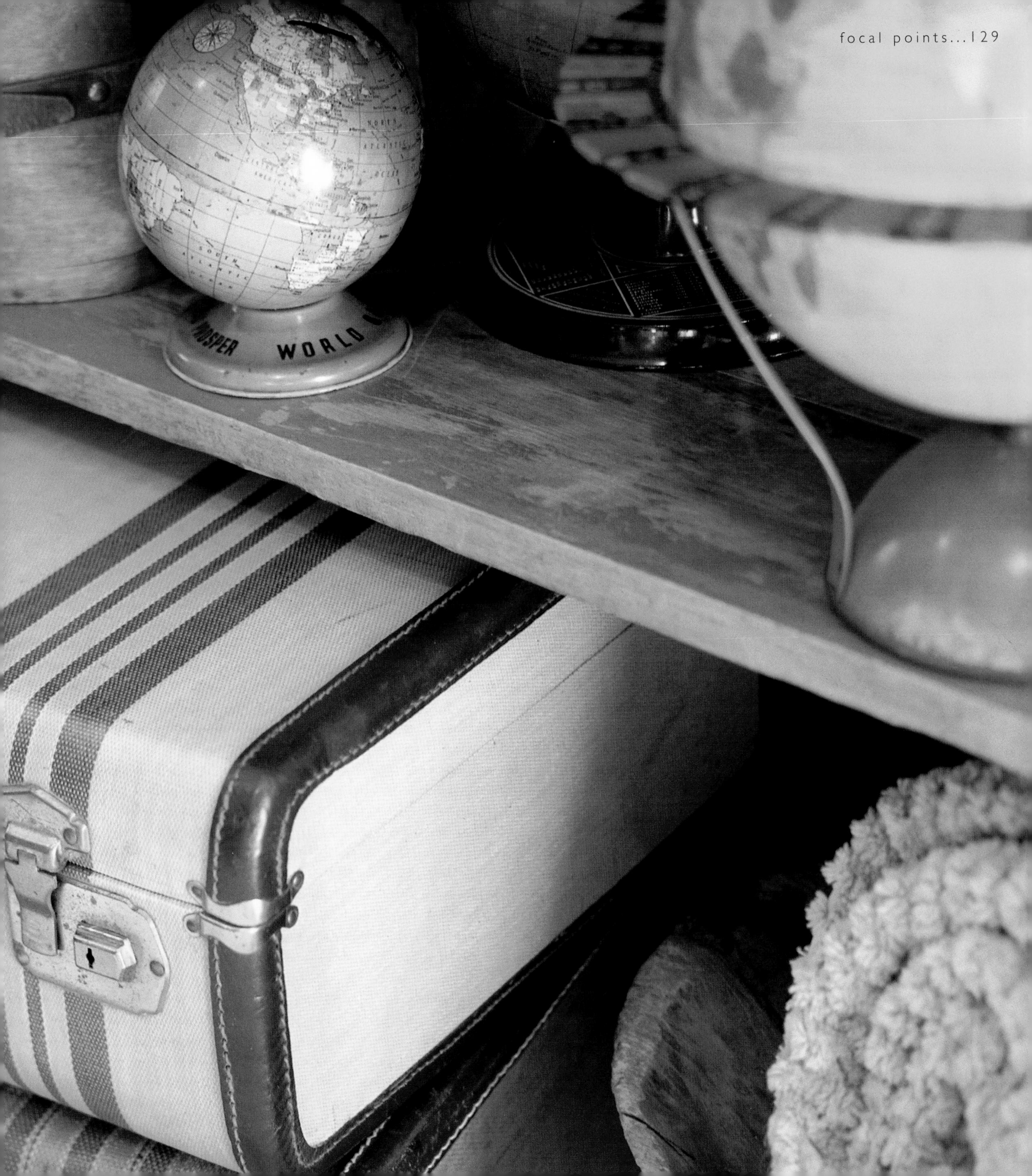
PROSPER
WORLD

Celebrate relationships, memories, and the connections between generations by bringing together in one spot your collection of photos of family and friends. The secret to this grouping's success is a tightly designed composition that incorporates both the tabletop and the wall. The garden table grounds the arrangement; the wrought-iron brackets define the width and height. Tall lamps, symmetrically placed, lead the eye from the tabletop to the brackets, framing a space that's filled by the architectural-salvage shelf and a picture centered between the lamps. On the table and shelves, frames in a mix of styles, shapes, and sizes cluster in companionable groupings, layered to create depth and draw the eye into and along the composition.

▲ In the kitchen, assemble a collage of family photos in coordinating frames to fill the space between cabinets and countertop.

◄ For a casual tabletop-wall display, start with a piece of salvaged fencing or metal like this screen-door protector. Prop snapshots on the piece, and use small easels and stacked books to showcase additional photos on the table below.

The quality o.

life is determined by the people in it.

Turn your hallway into a gallery that honors family and friends. For a unified look, choose identical frames and paint them, if necessary, to match the woodwork; paint the mats to match the wall. Use a computer to generate a stencil for the "caption" that runs along the wall below the photos (see page 182 for tips and instructions).

▲ Focal-point displays don't have to be permanent: A row of hats hung on pegs or a grid of straw hats on the wall is a fun and functional way to display attractive headgear when you're not wearing it. The arrangement works best as decoration if the hats blend with the dominant colors in the room. Oyster, cream, and taupe hues harmonize the hats with the pictures, the peg rack, and a small plate below them.

▶ Straw hats perfectly repeat the rich golden color of the pine armoire. Similar sunny wood tones in the orchard ladder, flooring, straw basket, and clay pot warm up white walls and help create a neutral-plus-white color scheme that's restful and relaxing. In addition, the harmony of honey tones keeps the hefty armoire from overwhelming the space.

Arrange a few of your favorite things where you can enjoy them up close. Objects that delight you because they resonate with meaning or have the patina of age offer a comforting familiarity that says "home." Here, antique sheep and wool needlework share desk space with an Early American inkwell.

▲ Objects whose shapes delight you often show to best advantage against a plain, contrasting background. Instead of lining them up like soldiers, bring every other one forward, creating depth. In this collection of new and antique teapots, turning one of them to face in the opposite direction adds a lighthearted touch of variety. The fifth object, a vase that's about the same height as the teapots, anchors the display, and three grasslike stems create a frame.

◄ Using the space under the table as well as on top gives you more room to arrange objects you enjoy looking at. The collection of baskets and containers also imparts greater visual weight to the table.

Early-20th-century doorknobs of smooth white porcelain, faceted glass, or intricately embossed brass recall an era that appreciated ornamentation and attention to detail. Piled in the tray of an antique scale (balanced by pocket change), the knobs arrest the eye and invite you to enjoy them as art.

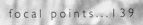

▲ Display collections of "smalls," as they're known in the antiques trade, in intimate groupings where they can be enjoyed at close range. Dollhouse dressers invite inspection on a bedside table.

◄ French, Dutch, and Italian opaline boxes, originally designed as cookie and candy containers, make a richly colorful show when stacked in front of leather-bound books.

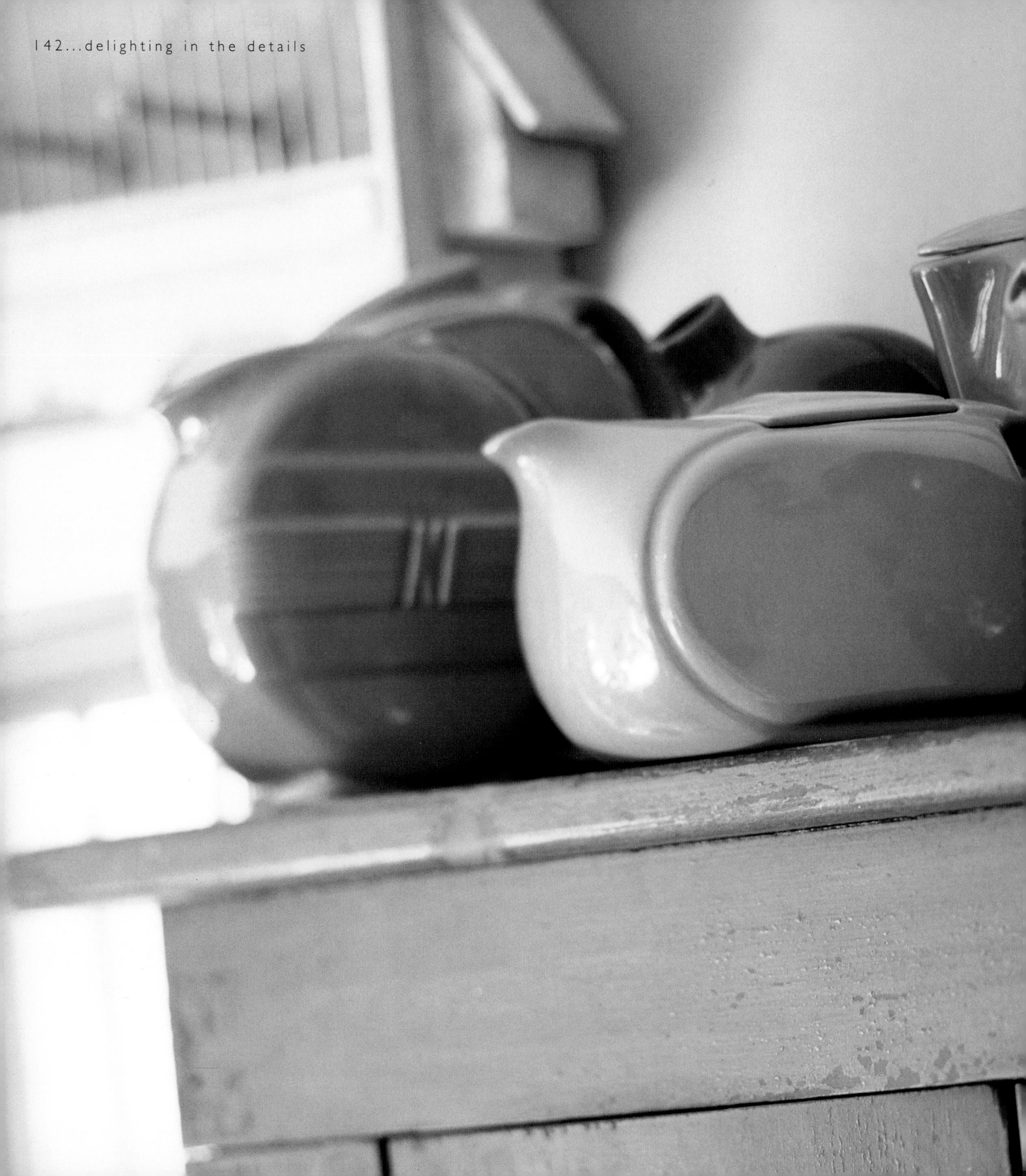

happy color

Lift your spirits with an eyeful of your favorite color. Lavender refrigerator pitchers from the first half of the 20th century are lined

up along the top of a blue-painted cupboard, where their bold hue gladdens the hearts of the collection's owners. You can achieve

similar impact with an assortment of objects unified by color—for example, yellow pitchers, vases, salt and pepper shakers, and

vintage napkins could be displayed in a cupboard or on a shelf for a splash of joyous hue.

◀ The mantel itself is a natural focal point in many homes, so it's the obvious location for assembling a collection of things you love. Lean paintings against the wall instead of hanging them if you like to change displays often. If you hang them, you'll have room to showcase objects on the mantel shelf; choose items that relate to the paintings in color, texture, or theme.

▲ Frame your children's artwork between thin sheets of acrylic plastic, letting the wall color serve as the mat. Plaster casts of the artists' hands, painted in bold primaries, decorate the mantel shelf.

◀ If a favorite painting is too small for the mantel by itself, give it more visual heft with a collection of related items. The weather vane fills out the left side of the mantel and supplies height, and the small bench and brackets lead the eye from the mantel shelf to the painting. Add objects as you like, choosing different shapes but limiting the colors to emphasize the painting.

treasure the past

Look for novel ways to display mementos. A cake

plate becomes a platform for showcasing a

daughter's first ballet shoes, protected from dust

by a glass dome, *opposite*. Pink seashells collected

on family vacations add a color accent around

the base and another prompt for memories.

Enjoy your collectibles by using them. A vintage

mirror and mirrored tray, *left*, combine to form

the centerpiece of a do-it-yourself dressing table.

Antique cosmetics containers add a luxurious

dimension to putting on makeup.

Unusual collections demand original display solutions. Hand mirrors with celluloid frames (dating from the 1880s to the 1920s) are grouped by color and size in a corner of the master bath, *opposite*. Those on the wall adjacent to the bathtub catch light from the window and bounce it into the room. White ironstone tureen lids, *right*, make an interesting variation on the practice of hanging collectible plates. Arranged with radial symmetry, they offer more dimension and variety of shape than plates or platters.

the tabletop

Whether you're eating a piece of toast by yourself or sitting down at the table with

the family, meals are—or should be—occasions to slow down and focus. You're

refueling the spirit as well as the body, and paying attention to details can enhance

the experience and make it more enjoyable. Bring special-occasion luxuries into

everyday use: Instead of scooping up cereal with a stainless-steel spoon, use a heavy

silver one picked up at an estate sale. Indulge your creativity with flourishes for the

table that make the ordinary occasion of dining (or breakfasting) feel extraordinary.

When you arrange food on the plate, notice the colors. A monochromatic meal may

taste fine, but a dollop of color makes it more appetizing.

fresh fruit

Savor the aroma and flavor of locally grown fresh fruit in season. The fact that the fruit is only available for a short time intensifies the pleasure it gives. Enjoy the beautiful colors and shapes of ripening peaches or tomatoes: Create a temporary still life, piling the fruits in a bowl or lining them up on the windowsill. Serve fruit salad from a tall compote, *opposite*, mixing dark and light colors as in a painting.

Cranberry Cheesecake Shake

Strawberry Gelato

Restaurants garnish dishes with sprigs of herbs or slices of fruit for a good reason: The splash of color enhances the appearance of the food, making the meal more appetizing because it pleases the eye. Garnishes also add contrasting texture or shape, so that the presentation becomes a work of art. And of course, garnishes are meant to complement the flavors of the food. A homemade cranberry cheesecake milk shake isn't complete until you top it with sugared cranberries, *opposite*. A sprig of oregano from the garden makes a surprising and piquant flavor mate for gelato and strawberries, *above*, and the color of the herb perks up the red of the strawberry slices. Taking the time to present food beautifully is an act of creativity and an expression of esteem for the people you're serving. (For recipes, see page 183.)

Greek-Style Shrimp Salad

Warm Fajita Salad

Express your inner artist in the way you set the table. Instead of ordinary place mats, use old breadboards (or even old books!) as a frame for the place setting. Layer fabrics, such as coarsely woven burlap and folded linen, *above,* to compose an abstract grid underlying the plate. Even spreading a dinner napkin on the diagonal, allowing one corner to drape over the table edge, presents the plate with distinction. Flatware that feels good in the hand also makes eating more pleasurable. Look for old restaurant silverware at flea markets and antiques shops, and mix and match styles for an interesting table setting. (For recipes, see pages 183–184.)

places, everyone

Pasta with Ricotta and Vegetables

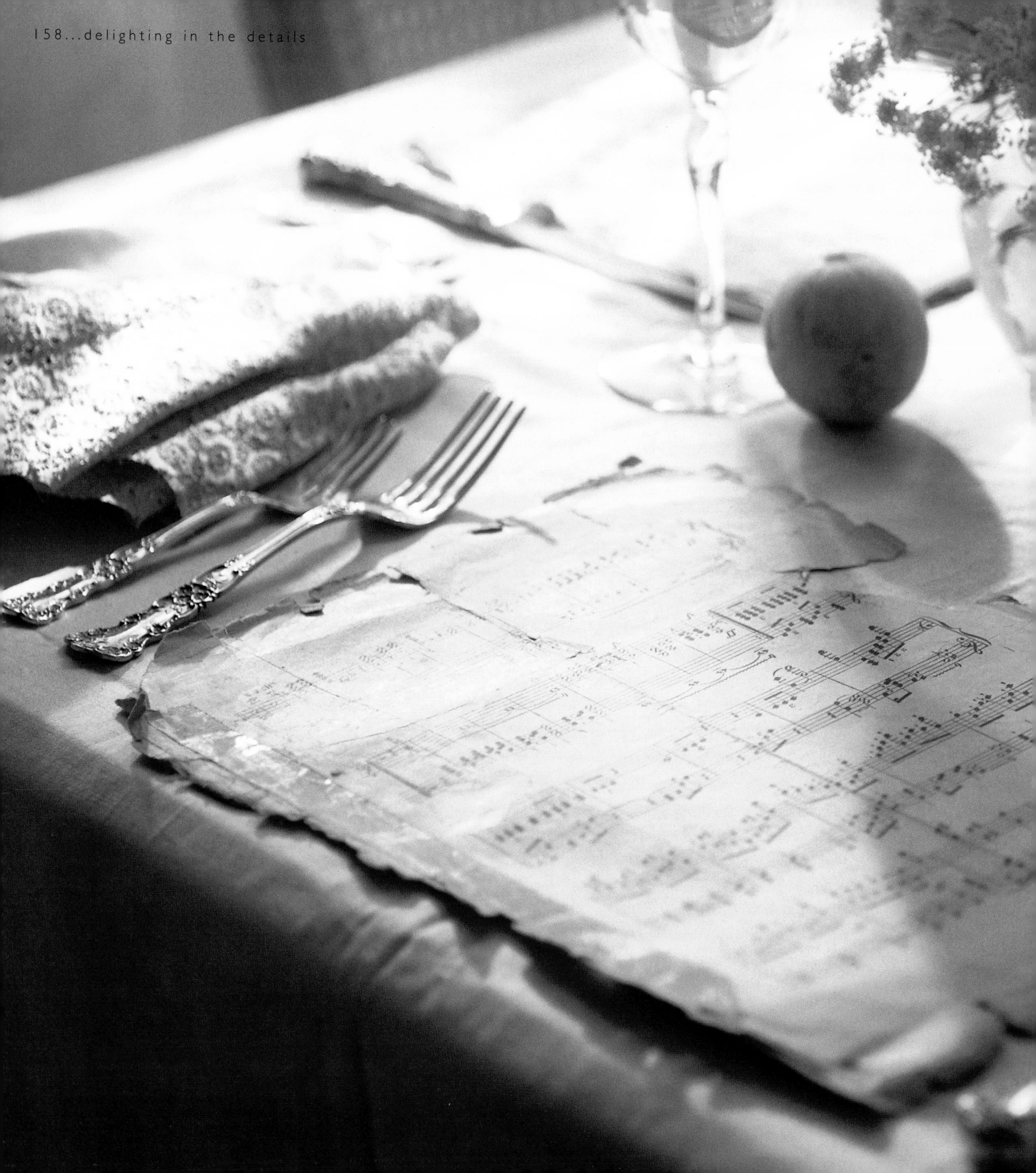

Sheet music from a church garage sale makes fun place mats for a music-loving family. You might also find sheet music at charity book sales, thrift stores, or yard sales. If you don't want to risk staining the sheet music, make photocopies and tea-stain them for a softer, aged appearance. To tea-stain paper, brew a cup of strong tea, leaving the tea bag in the cup. When the tea is lukewarm, use the tea bag as a sponge and wipe it over the paper. Let the paper dry. The edges of the paper will curl as it dries, but you can flatten the paper by placing it under a stack of books for about a day.

comfort foods

Rhubarb-Raspberry-Apple Pie

Cherry Puff

Exactly what constitutes comfort food is very personal—for one person, it's a cheeseburger and fries; for another, it's Grandma's apple pie. Whatever your favorites happen to be, make them even more special with embellishments and presentation. Instead of a solid or lattice crust, for example, top a pie with pastry cutouts, *above*. Brushing the pastry with milk and sprinkling it with sugar before baking makes the cutouts sparkly and festive. Rather than baking cobblers in a large dish or casserole, use individual custard cups for cozy single-serving treats, *opposite*. (For recipes, see page 185.)

Setting a pretty table shows friends that you put some thought into creating a welcoming environment. Keep it simple to lower

your own stress level, but have fun with it too. Place cards let you mix up seating patterns and guide people to where you want

them to go. To make a card like the one *above*, string baby-bracelet beads onto jewelry wire (both available from a crafts store).

Punch holes in a folded card and run the wire through the holes, curling the wire ends. For the centerpiece, a low mound of

flowers, leaves, or berries is best—it provides a focal point for the table but won't interfere with conversation. If you have flow-

ers blooming, use those. Otherwise, buy a dozen roses from a florist a day or two ahead of the dinner and let them open up

slightly. To encourage them, cut the stem ends at an angle and stand them in warm water. For the container, use a small casse-

role dish or another low, wide-mouth container. Fill it with wet florist's foam (from a crafts store). Cut the stems to 3 to 4

inches and insert them in the foam so the blossoms form a low mound. Tuck in leaves, allowing some to fall over the rim.

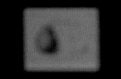

For a casual gathering, leave the tablecloths in the linen closet and use place mats on bare wood. Service plates, which are 12 inches in diameter, are popular for informal dining (a standard dinner plate is 10 inches in diameter). Top service plates with rimmed bowls for salad or soup, or with smaller serving plates. Using votive candles instead of tapers keeps warm light low, out of the line of vision between guests. If you have flowers left over from the centerpiece, stand single blossoms in juice glasses or small votive holders and set one at each place.

center of attention

Turn table decorating into creative play by working with what you have on hand. Use a platter, charger, or tray to unify the items. For a summertime table, *opposite*, stand three bottles on a charger and insert tall stems of delphinium (or any other tall, spiky flower). Add large seashells and sea glass around the base of the bottles. Assemble a tabletop water garden, *left*, using a 19-inch terra-cotta saucer for the base. Fill a shallow, glazed terra-cotta bowl with river rocks and water. Arrange small potted plants around the bowl and use clean clay saucers for condiments.

Dress up chairs as well as the table with table runners, *opposite*. Use purchased runners or sew your own. If you use purchased ones, drape the runner over the chair back and tack ribbons to the edges near the seat so you can tie the cover in place. If you sew your own, choose washable fabric for easy care. Make the rectangle slightly narrower than the chair back and as long as you like. For a variation on a place mat that protects the tabletop without hiding it, use folded cotton dish towels. Embellish them with stamped designs, using fruit as your stamp (see page 181 for instructions).

1   If napkin rings are jewelry for the table, why not use the real thing? Make a birthday dinner memorable with creative table decorations. Roll up napkins and slip them through chunky bracelets for each place setting.   2   Bring out your necklaces and drape them around hurricane shades for the centerpiece. Strings of inexpensive glass beads work well too, catching the light from the candles.

Simple touches

Napkin rings add style to the table

setting, but you don't need anything

fancy or elaborate. Tying a ribbon

around each napkin and tucking a leaf

into the knot supplies a touch of grace.

breakfast in bed

Surprise your mate (or your kids) with a love note at breakfast. Make your own note holder using an alligator clip and lead-free silver solder from a hardware store (see page 181 for instructions). Or use photo clips (similar to this one, but usually anchored in a plastic cube or metal cone); they're available at discount stores and specialty gift shops.

Embark on the day at a more relaxed pace. Why not start with breakfast in bed? A sturdy lap tray with short legs makes a practical table for transporting coffee or tea from the kitchen to the bedroom. Or take breakfast out on the porch and enjoy the sounds and scents of a new day's beginning.

project instructions

Candle Sack
Designed by Sonja Carmen

Materials
- ⅝ yard of sheer organza in the color of your choice
- paper for pattern
- pencil and straightedge
- dressmaker's pins
- sewing machine
- iron
- assorted metal beads
- needle and thread

Referring to the diagram, use the straightedge to draw a pattern on paper. Use a book to make sure the four inner angles of the cross shape are right angles.

Pin the pattern to the fabric, and cut around the pattern edges. Press each arm of the cross toward the center (along the broken line indicated on the diagram) to define a square at the center of the cross. This will be the bottom of the candle sack.

With right sides facing, pin together two adjacent arms of the cross and stitch, using a ¼-inch seam allowance. Repeat to join all the arms, forming a box-shape sack. Press the seams and turn the sack right side out.

Fold the top edge to the inside ½ inch and press. Fold again to make a double hem; the depth of the second fold will determine the height of the candle sack. Topstitch close to both folded edges.

Hand-sew beads around the hemmed top edge of the sack. Insert a votive candleholder or glass pillar candleholder and candle. Use a long match to light the candle, being careful to keep the flame away from the sack.

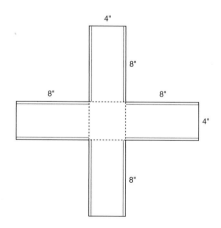

Jelly-Jar Hanging Candle
Designed by Carrie Hansen

Materials
- short jelly jar with raised edge or lip
- 18-gauge steel wire (from a hardware store)
- needlenose pliers
- assorted beads (choose beads with holes large enough to receive the wire)
- candle wax and wick (from a crafts store)

Cut a piece of wire long enough to wrap around the jelly jar below the lip, with ⅝ inch to spare. Fold the wire in half and twist tightly about 5/16 inch below the fold to make a loop. Wrap the wire around the jar and twist the ends tightly, then twist the free ends to make a second loop.

Cut four 2-inch-long pieces of wire. Use needlenose pliers to twist one end of each piece into a loop; slide beads onto each piece. Thread the straight end of each piece through one of the loops on the side of the jar. Curl the wire end to secure the strands of beads.

For the hanger, cut wire to the desired length and bend it into a horseshoe shape. Slip each end under the wire around the jelly jar and curl the ends.

Melt the wax according to the manufacturer's instructions and pour into the jar. Stand a piece of wick in the hot wax and let cool.

Vellum-Wrapped Topiary
Designed by Steed Hale

Materials
- cone-shape topiary form
- kraft paper or newspaper
- marking pen, tape
- vellum (available from art supply stores)
- double-stick tape
- acrylic prism with pull-chain (available at lighting stores)

Make a paper pattern as described for Tomato-Cage Luminaria (page 173).

Trim away the top of the pattern so the top third of the topiary form will be exposed. Trim the bottom edge even with or slightly lower than the bottom ring of the form.

Lay the pattern on the vellum and lightly trace around it. Cut out the vellum. Apply double-stick tape to one vertical edge and wrap the vellum snugly around the topiary form. Press the remaining vertical edge onto the double-stick tape.

Loop the end of the pull-chain around the top of the topiary so the prism dangles in the center (see photo). Place votive candles under the topiary. Choose votive candleholders that are 2 or 3 inches taller than the candle to protect the flame from breezes. Never leave burning candles unattended.

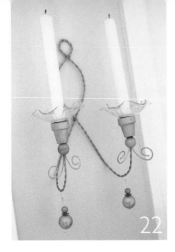

Wire and Bead Candle Sconce
Designed by Peggy Johnston

Materials
- 14-gauge galvanized steel wire (from a hardware store)
- pliers, wire cutters
- heavy-duty tape
- vise
- electric drill and cup hook
- 20-gauge wire (from a hardware or crafts store)
- silver spray paint
- 2 wooden "flowerpots" 1¼×1⅜ inches (from a crafts store)
- assorted beads, including two 1-inch-diameter wooden beads and two ⅞-inch-diameter wooden beads
- 2 brass grommets ⅞-inch diameter (from a crafts store)
- 24-gauge silver wire (from a crafts store)
- 5-minute epoxy (optional)

Cut a 6-foot length of the galvanized steel wire and fold it in half. You will use the electric drill to twist the folded wire.

Use heavy-duty tape to tape the wire ends together; then clamp the taped ends in the vise. At least 2 inches of the wire ends should be held in the vise.

To insert the cup hook in the drill, remove the bit, insert the screw end of the cup hook, and tighten the drill. Catch the cup hook over the folded center of the galvanized wire and slowly press the drill trigger so that the wire twists tightly on itself. When the twists approach the cup hook, stop and insert a 2½-inch-long piece of wood or heavy cardboard to keep the wire from twisting all the way up to the hook. Continue twisting up to this point; then slip the hook out.

Trim the untwisted ends of the wire (which were in the vise). Find the center of the twisted wire and loop it around a broom handle or 1-inch-diameter dowel to make the hanging loop. Cross the wires at the base of this loop and secure them by wrapping tightly with 20-gauge wire. Twist the ends of the 20-gauge wire at the back of the loop and trim to ½ inch.

About 4½ inches from the base of the hanging loop, cross and shape the wire to form an elongated oval that's pointed at both ends. Secure the crossed wires as directed above.

Bend and shape the ends of the wire forward and up to form two arms.

Spray the wooden flowerpots and beads silver. Slip one 1-inch bead onto each arm. Slip one flowerpot onto each arm. Inside the flowerpot, untwist the wires and spread them to form a Y pressing against the sides of the flowerpot. Trim the wire ends to ½ inch.

Press a grommet into each flowerpot to provide a nonflammable interior for the candle to rest in. String beads and the ⅞-inch-diameter wooden beads onto pieces of 24-gauge silver wire and wrap the wires around the arms of the sconce. Cut four 4-inch lengths of 20-gauge wire and make curlicues. Push two curlicues into each bead under the flowerpots. If any of the parts seem unstable, use 5-minute epoxy to secure them.

Tomato-Cage Luminaria
Designed by Steed Hale

Materials
- cone-shape tomato cage (from a garden center)
- wire cutters
- metal file
- kraft paper or newspaper
- marking pen, tape
- aluminum screen (from a hardware store)
- 1×1-inch hardware cloth (available at hardware stores)
- gold and silver metallic spray paints
- 1½-inch-long safety pins (you'll need about 500)

Using wire cutters, trim the legs from the tomato cage so the widest wire circle rests flat. Smooth off sharp edges with the metal file.

To make a pattern for the screen covering, wrap kraft paper or newspaper snugly around the cage and tape it in place. Tape pieces of paper together as necessary to cover the form. Fold the excess paper over the top and bottom edges, creasing to make a clear edge. Draw a vertical line from top to bottom to mark the side seam. Carefully remove the pattern from the cage and cut away the excess paper at top and bottom along the creased lines.

Lay the pattern on the aluminum screen and trace around it, adding ½ inch along each vertical edge to allow for overlap at the side seam. Repeat to cut the shape from hardware cloth.

Protect your work area with newspapers and work on one side of each shape at a time. Spray both sides of the aluminum screen silver; spray both sides of the hardware cloth gold. After the paint dries, lay the hardware cloth over the aluminum screen and wrap both around the cage.

Using safety pins, pin the hardware cloth and screen to the top and bottom rungs of the tomato cage, packing the pins as tightly as possible. Secure the side seam with pins as well.

Pleated Paper Shade Slipcover
Designed by Peggy Johnston

Materials
- temporary shade such as **Redi-Shade** (available at home improvement centers and home decorating stores)
- straightedge
- crafts knife
- acrylic paints in the desired colors
- ¼-inch round pointed artist's paintbrushes
- ¼-inch round paper punch
- 1 yard of ⅜-inch-wide ribbon

Measure the height of the lampshade from top edge to bottom edge and add 1 inch.

Using a straightedge and crafts knife, trim the pleated shade to this length. Work with the shade folded; you may have to make several cuts to trim all the way through the pleats.

Stretch the shade out, holding it in place with books or other weights. Using the paintbrushes and acrylic paints, apply the design of your choice along one edge. Thin the paints slightly with water if needed.

After the paint dries, repleat the shade. Working with a few pleats at a time, punch holes through the shade along the unpainted edge. Center one hole on each

pleat panel and position it about ½ inch from the edge. Once you have the first holes punched, use them as a guide for the remaining holes, but check the positioning from time to time to make sure the holes are correctly placed.

Cut off one pleat panel at the end without the self-adhesive tape. Remove the backing from the taped edge and press the two ends together, forming a pleated cylinder. Thread ribbon through the holes and carefully draw up the top of the cylinder until it fits the top edge of the existing shade. Tie the ribbon in a bow to secure the pleats.

Lavender Sachet
Designed by Carrie Hansen

Materials
- two 4¼×6½-inch rectangles of ticking fabric
- two 4¼×6½-inch rectangles of sheer organza for lining
- 1 yard of ⅜-inch-wide velvet ribbon
- lavender buds or sprigs

Place one ticking rectangle on one lining rectangle, right sides facing. Cut a 7-inch length of velvet ribbon and fold it in half. Lay the folded ribbon between the ticking and the lining on one 4¼-inch edge, raw edges aligned. Stitch the lining, ticking, and ribbon ends together along the

short edge, using a ¼-inch seam allowance. Stitch the remaining ticking and lining rectangles together along one short edge, right sides facing.

Turn each lining/ticking unit to the right side (wrong sides facing) and press the top edge. Stack the units with the right sides of the ticking facing. Stitch the units together along the sides and bottom, using a ¼-inch seam allowance. Trim the seam allowances close to the stitching.

Align the bottom seam with one side seam and stitch across the bottom corner, perpendicular to the seams, to make a boxlike edge. Repeat for the opposite bottom corner.

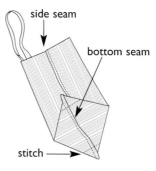

About ½ inch from the top edge, remove the stitches from each side seam for about 1 inch. Turn the sachet to the right side. Add lavender, keeping the buds below the openings in the seams.

Cut two pieces of ribbon 13 inches long. Fold one ribbon in half and thread it through the bag. Pass the remaining ribbon through the fold and tie a bow to secure it (see the diagram *below*). To close the bag, pull the free ends of the first ribbon, gathering the bag shut. Tie the ribbon ends in a bow.

Lavender Buckwheat Hull Pillow
Designed by Peggy Johnston

Materials
- purchased buckwheat pillow
- stiff paper
- 2 cups of lavender buds
- needle and thread
- pillowcase and coordinating ribbon or lace

Carefully remove the stitches from one seam of the buckwheat pillow. Roll the stiff paper into a cone to use as a funnel; pour the lavender buds into the pillow.

With needle and thread, stitch the seam closed. Shake the pillow to distribute the lavender buds among the buckwheat hulls.

Embellish a purchased pillowcase with ribbon or lace, stitching it around the hem at the opening. Insert the lavender-buckwheat pillow.

Tranquillity Pillow
Designed by Peggy Johnston

Materials
- vintage handkerchief
- embroidery needle and embroidery threads in desired colors (optional)
- coordinating or contrasting fabric
- sewing machine, threads to match fabrics
- 2 cups of lavender buds

The finished size of the pillow will be barely larger than the handkerchief. If desired, embroider a design in the corners of the handkerchief. Purple French knots and leaves outlined with straight stitches emphasize the cutwork motif of the handkerchief in the photo.

From coordinating or contrasting fabric, cut two squares ½ inch larger all around than the handkerchief. With right sides facing, stitch the squares together using a ¼-inch seam; leave an opening on one side for turning. Turn to the right side and press.

Fill the pillow with lavender. Hand-stitch the opening closed. If the handkerchief has a wide border, mark and stitch a similar one on the pillow. Also topstitch ¼ inch from the pillow's edge all the way around.

Center the handkerchief on the pillow, making sure that about ¼ inch of the pillow shows all around. Stitch the handkerchief to the pillow, using white thread in the needle and thread to match the pillow in the bobbin.

Ballerina Night-Light
Designed by Peggy Johnston

Materials
(most supplies can be found at a hardware store or home improvement center)
- 4 glass marbles
- ⅜-inch galvanized floor flange (for the base)
- 5-minute epoxy
- ¾ × 5-inch galvanized steel pipe nipple (this is the threaded pipe that forms the body of the night-light)
- wire cutters, utility knife
- 6-foot cord set with candelabra base snap-in socket and switch
- 1½ × ⅜-inch lamp nipple
- 2-inch keyless candelabra base socket
- silver spray paint
- tissue paper from an art supply store
- 22-gauge wire
- candelabra bulb
- needle and thread to match the tissue paper

Using 5-minute epoxy, glue the marbles to the underside of the floor flange, spacing them evenly. Screw one end of the pipe nipple into the floor flange.

Screw the lamp nipple into the keyless candelabra base socket.

Cut off the socket on the 6-foot cord/switch set. Thread the cut end of the cord up through the floor flange and pipe nipple assembly to the top of the pipe nipple. Slide the lamp nipple with the candelabra base socket over the cut end of the cord. Insert the lamp nipple into the pipe nipple so the base of the socket rests on the top of the pipe nipple.

Remove the cardboard cover from the candelabra socket. Spray the cardboard cover silver.

With a utility knife, slit the last 2 inches of the cord's plastic casing along the indentation. Do not cut

the wires inside. Cut away the plastic casing to expose about 1 inch of wire. Notice that one half of the casing leads back to the wide prong on the plug and one leads to the narrow prong. Follow the casing from plug to cut end and attach the wires from the wide prong to the silver screw on the socket. To do this, curl the wires around the screw and tighten it. Attach the remaining wires to the gold screw in the same way. Slide the cardboard cover over the socket.

To make the shade, cut a 9-inch circle of tissue paper. Crumple the paper to give it texture and then flatten it again. In the center of the paper circle, draw a 1¼-inch-diameter circle. Cut small slits from the center of this smaller circle to the drawn edge. The slits will fold down over the wire frame.

To make the frame, bend one end of the 22-gauge wire into a small loop; then spiral the wire around the top two-thirds of the candelabra bulb, leaving the excess wire at the top of the spiral. Wrap the wire just above the spiral around a 1⅛-inch-diameter object such as the cap of a shampoo bottle to form a circle. Cut the wire.

Center the tissue paper shade over the wire circle and fold the slitted sections over the wire. Using a needle and thread, hand-stitch paper over the wire to secure it. Make a second row of stitches about ¼ inch from the first to suggest a "neck" on the lampshade.

Insert the bulb into the socket and rest the shade on the bulb.

Millstone fountain
Designed by Hermann Weis

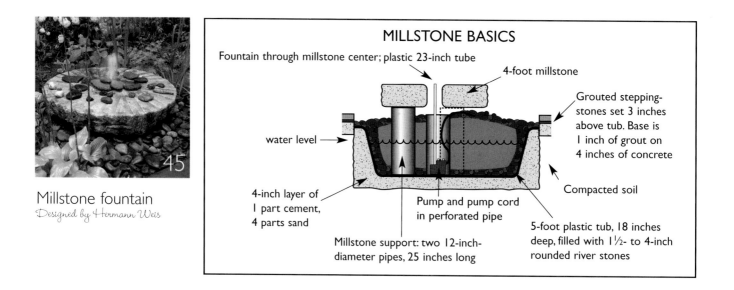

MILLSTONE BASICS

Fountain through millstone center; plastic 23-inch tube

4-foot millstone

Grouted stepping-stones set 3 inches above tub. Base is 1 inch of grout on 4 inches of concrete

water level

4-inch layer of 1 part cement, 4 parts sand

Pump and pump cord in perforated pipe

Millstone support: two 12-inch-diameter pipes, 25 inches long

Compacted soil

5-foot plastic tub, 18 inches deep, filled with 1½- to 4-inch rounded river stones

45

55

Fabric Columns
Designed by Steed Hale

Materials
- 4 lace panels at least 48 inches wide and long enough to reach from ceiling to floor plus 2 inches (if necessary, piece panels to obtain the width for desired fullness)
- fringe
- sewing thread
- four 12×12-inch flat L-shape corner braces (from a hardware store)
- plumb bob, awl
- screws, toggle bolts, or expansion screws for attaching braces
- screwdriver

On the top edge of each lace panel, turn under ½ inch, then 1½ inches and stitch close to the lower folded edge to make a rod pocket.

Stitch fringe to the remaining three sides of each lace panel.

Slide a corner brace into the rod pocket on each panel, gathering the fabric toward the corner.

Using a plumb bob, drop a line from the ceiling to the floor so the string reaches just beyond the corner of the bed. On the ceiling, mark this spot as the inside corner of the brace. Place the brace flat against the ceiling and mark the positions of the brace's screw holes. Use an awl to make a pilot hole at each mark, then screw the brace to the ceiling, using long screws, toggle bolts, or expansion screws. Repeat for the remaining corners. If desired, carefully paint the exposed braces to match the ceiling.

Scarf Canopy
Designed by Gina Harrell

Materials
- chiffon scarves of various sizes and coordinating patterns
- chiffon fabric
- thread to match fabrics
- sewing machine
- 4 eye screws
- monofilament (available at crafts stores)

To determine the size of the canopy top, measure the length and width of the bed and add 8 to 12 inches to each measurement (depending on the desired amount of drape). You will also need a floor-length solid panel at the head of the bed and six 12- to 18-inch-wide corner curtains. The width of the solid panel should be about 8 inches wider than the bed. To determine the length of the curtains, measure the distance from floor to ceiling and subtract 12 inches. The width of the curtains will be determined by the width of your scarves.

For the canopy top, spread the largest scarves out on the bed to determine the best placement. Cut shapes from coordinating chiffon fabric as needed to fill in the canopy. Sew narrow rolled hems on the chiffon pieces. Then sew the scarves and chiffon pieces together, overlapping the edges ¼ inch and using a wide zigzag stitch. You may need to adjust your machine's thread tension and use a new, fine needle to keep the fabric from puckering.

Repeat the procedure to assemble the corner curtains and head panel; then stitch them to the canopy top, attaching one corner curtain on each side of the head panel and two at each corner that will hang above the end of the bed.

Install eye screws in the ceiling over the corners of the bed. Stitch monofilament to each corner of the canopy and tie the monofilament to the eye screw.

Fleece-Covered Hot Water Bottle
Designed by Peggy Johnston

Materials
- hot water bottle
- paper for pattern
- compass
- ⅓ yard of fleece
- thread to match fabric
- sewing machine
- embroidery thread and needle
- ribbon to match fabric

To make a pattern for the cover, lay the hot water bottle on the paper and trace around it. Add ½ inch all around for the pattern. (This will be the seam line.)

Using a compass, draw scallops along the sides and bottom edge of the pattern, using the seam line as the baseline. Do not draw scallops along the top 4 inches on each side. This will be gathered by a ribbon when finished.

Fold the fabric, selvage edges together. Position the pattern's top edge on the selvage edge of the fleece and cut two matching pieces.

With wrong sides facing, stitch the cover together along the seam line, leaving the top edge open. Trim the seam allowances at the neck to ¼ inch.

Using an embroidery needle and thread, blanket-stitch around the scallop edges and across the selvage edges at the neck.

Insert the water bottle and tie the neck closed with ribbon.

73

Terry Cloth Slipcover
Designed by Carrie Hansen

Materials
- camp-style wooden folding chair
- sewing machine

For seat:
- 2½-inch-thick upholstery foam
- electric knife or utility knife
- two large bath towels
- four 1×12-inch strips of fabric for ties
- fabric and ¼-inch-diameter cording for piping

For chair back:
- two 17¼×2-inch strips of contrasting fabric for trim
- 37½×16-inch towel
- four 1×12-inch strips of fabric for ties

SEAT CUSHION
With an electric knife or utility knife, cut the upholstery foam to fit the chair seat (the one shown is 14 inches square).

From the large towels, cut three skirt panels: Cut two 14¼×6-inch side panels from one towel, using the finished borders (top and bottom edges) as the lower edge of each skirt panel and one finished side edge of the towel as a finished side edge of each skirt panel. Cut a 14×6-inch front panel from the second towel in the same manner. To finish the remaining side edge on each panel, fold ¾ inch to the wrong side and stitch.

From the remaining fabric in the two large towels, cut a 15-inch square top panel. Also cut a 9×15-inch panel and an 11×15-inch panel for the cushion bottom; and four strips 3½×15 inches for the gussets (sides).

For piping, from contrasting fabric, cut enough bias strips to cover a 60-inch length of cording. (To make piping, cut 1½-inch-wide strips diagonally across the fabric. Join the strips at the short ends with ¼-inch seams to make one long continuous strip. Fold the fabric, wrong sides together, around the cording and stitch close to the cording, using a zipper foot.)

To make the ties, from contrasting fabric, cut four 1×12-inch strips along the straight grain of the fabric. Fold each strip in half lengthwise, right sides facing, and stitch one short end and the long edge, using a ¼-inch seam allowance. Turn the tube to the right side and press.

Starting in one back corner of the top panel, pin the piping to the right side of the top panel, raw edges aligned, and baste in place, stitching close to the piping. Pin one pair of ties in each back corner, raw edges aligned. Pin the skirt panels to the top panel, right sides facing and sandwiching the piping and ties in between. Center each skirt panel on the top panel edge (the corner of the cushion will show between the side and front skirts). Stitch through all layers, using a ½-inch seam allowance.

For the sides or gusset of the seat cushion, stitch the four side strips together at the short ends, using a ½-inch seam allowance.

Lay the two bottom panels, right sides faceup, so the edges overlap to form a 15-inch square. Pin them together to make assembly easier. Pin the gusset to the bottom panels, right sides facing and raw edges aligned, clipping the gusset seam allowance at the corners. Stitch the gusset to the bottom panels. Remove the pins holding the flap in place.

With right sides facing, pin the gusset to the top panel. The skirt panels and ties will be sandwiched between the top and bottom panels. Stitch. Turn to the right side through the bottom flap. Insert the upholstery foam.

BACK
From fabric, cut two 17¼×2-inch strips. Fold under ¼ inch along each long edge. Pin one strip over the decorative border at one end of the towel (or 3½ inches from the edge of the towel if there is no decorative border). Pin the remaining strip over the border at the opposite end of the towel, on the back side of the towel (which will fold up to make pockets and become the "right" side of the chair back). Fold the excess of each strip to the opposite side of the towel. Stitch close to the long folded edges of each strip.

Fold one end of the towel up about 10 inches. (Both fabric trims will now be on the "right" side of the towel.) Divide the width of the towel into thirds and make two lines of stitching from the bottom edge of the decorative border to the finished edge of the towel.

Fold under the sides of the towel ¾ inch to 1 inch, if necessary, to fit the width of the chair back. Stitch.

Make four ties (see above under Seat Cushion). Stitch one tie to each corner of the chair back cover. Fold the cover over the chair back and tie in place.

Spa Pillow
Designed by Carrie Hansen

Materials
- purchased bath pillow with suction cups (the one shown is 14¼ inches long and 5 inches in diameter)
- sewing machine, threads to match fabrics
- white bath towel
- stencils or computer-generated type for the word "relax"
- spray glue
- adhesive-backed shelf paper
- aqua hand towel (or color of your choice)
- crafts glue (optional)
- aqua gingham (or color to match hand towel)
- ¼-inch-wide white satin ribbon

From the white towel, cut a 15×20-inch panel. Turn under 2 inches on each short end to make a hem; stitch.

Using stencils or computer-generated type, transfer the letters for the word "relax" to paper (the letters shown are 2½ inches high). Cut them out and spray-glue them to the adhesive-backed shelf paper; cut out again. Peel the backing from the shelf paper and press the letters onto the aqua towel. Cut the letters from the towel. Remove the shelf paper and position the letters on the white towel panel, centering the word. Use a dab of crafts glue to

tack each letter in place.

Using the satin stitch on your sewing machine, sew each letter to the pillow (white) panel.

On the 2-inch hem at each end of the pillow panel, mark the placement of the suction cups. Make buttonholes at these marks.

From gingham, cut two panels 4×14½ inches. Fold each panel in half, right sides facing and matching short ends. Stitch the short ends together with a ¼-inch seam allowance. On one long edge of each loop, fold the fabric under ¼ inch, then ¾ inch. Stitch close to the second fold to make a casing for the drawstring. Leave a small opening to insert the drawstring.

With right sides facing, fold the pillow panel so the buttonholes align. Pin the hemmed edges together. Pin and stitch one gingham loop to each end of the towel panel, right sides facing. Remove the pins in the hemmed edges and turn the cover to the right side.

Thread ribbon through the casing at each end of the pillow and draw up tightly. Tie in a bow. Insert the spa pillow, pulling the suction cups through the buttonholes.

Seasonal Pillow Covers
Designed by Molly Pashibin
Created by Sonja Carmon

Corduroy Pillow Materials
- standard 18-inch square pillow form
- ⅔ yard 54-inch-wide upholstery-weight plum corduroy
- ⅓ yard pink waffle corduroy
- 5¼-inch square of tan waleless corduroy
- sewing machine, threads to match fabrics
- 4 tassels
- decorative button

From the plum corduroy, cut one back panel 12×19 inches, one back panel 16×19 inches, and two 7¾×12-inch rectangles. From the pink corduroy, cut two 8×12-inch rectangles.

To assemble the patchwork front, stitch the rectangles to the tan corduroy square and to each other in the order shown in the diagram, using ½-inch seam allowances. The assembled cover should measure 19 inches square.

To assemble the envelope-style back, turn under one short edge of each back panel 1 inch and stitch. Place the patchwork front faceup; layer the back panels facedown on the front, overlapping the hemmed edges (the overlap will be deep) so that the outside edges align with the outside edges

of the patchwork front. Pin and stitch through all layers all the way around, using ½-inch seam allowances. Turn to the right side through the envelope opening.

Hand-stitch one tassel in each corner. Stitch a decorative button to the center of the square.

Sheer Slipcover Materials
- 18-inch square pillow
- 1½ yards 45-inch-wide printed sheer fabric
- thread to match fabric
- sewing machine
- six ⅝-inch-diameter plastic rings (like those used for making Roman shades)
- tassel

Cut two sheer rectangles 25½×29¾ inches. Hem the edges, turning the fabric under ¼ inch twice and stitching close to the fold.

Spread one panel on a flat surface, wrong side up. Center the pillow on the panel. Spread the second panel over the pillow, right side up. Working on one corner at a time, draw the corners of both panels through a plastic ring until the panels fit the pillow loosely. Gather up the fabric at the center of the front panel and draw it through a plastic ring to tighten the panel over the front of the pillow. Repeat on the back. Adjust the corners and centers as needed until you're happy with the fit. Tie a tassel around the center pouf on the front.

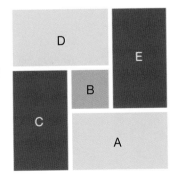

Corner Shelf Unit

Materials
- louvered bifold shutters
- 2×¾-inch wood strip
- ¾-inch plywood
- table saw
- wood glue
- 1½-inch finish nails
- 2-inch or 2½-inch wood screws

Look for pairs of bifold shutters at a home center. The height of the shutters will determine the size of the cabinet.

Lay the shutters flat on a work surface. Cut two pieces of 2×¾-inch wood strip the same length as the shutters. Lay one piece on each side of a shutter. Measure across the wood pieces and shutters and add ⅛ inch to allow for the shutters to open and close properly. The resulting measurement equals the total width of the cabinet front. (For example, if each bifold shutter when open and lying flat is 15 inches wide, the cabinet front would be 30 inches plus 4 inches for the 2-inch-wide wood pieces plus ⅛-inch clearance for a total of 34⅛ inches.)

To make the top and bottom of the cabinet, center the front

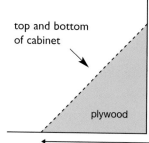

top and bottom of cabinet

plywood

total-width measurement across one corner of a piece of ¾-inch plywood, making sure the two sides are equal. Draw a line from side to side to mark the long edge of the triangle. Cut two pieces this size.

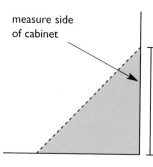

measure side of cabinet

Measure the side of the triangle for the top or bottom piece. Cut two pieces of ¾-inch plywood to this width and 1½ inches shorter than the height of the shutters. These will be the cabinet sides.

Glue and nail the two side pieces together along one edge using a butt joint (this will fit into the corner of your room). Attach the top and bottom pieces.

Determine the number of shelves desired and measure inside the cabinet to determine the dimensions. Cut the shelves to this size and install, using wood glue and 1½-inch finish nails.

Using wood glue and 1½-inch finish nails, attach the 2-inch trim pieces to the front edges of the cabinet sides. Attach the shutters to the trim. Paint the shutters and cabinet unit and attach to wall studs using 2-inch or 2½-inch screws.

106

Underbed Storage Box
Designed by Carrie Hansen

Materials
- two 7¼×21½-inch pieces of ¾-inch plywood for front and back of the box
- two 7¼×30-inch pieces of ¾-inch plywood for sides
- two 20×30-inch pieces of ¼-inch plywood for the lid and bottom
- two 20-inch lengths of ½×1½-inch wood strips and two 27-inch lengths of ½×1½-inch wood strips for the bottom frame
- four 6½-inch pieces quarter-round molding
- wood glue
- 1½-inch-long wood screws
- ¾-inch finish nails
- wood buttons (to cover the screw heads)
- sandpaper
- drill and drill bits, including 1½-inch paddle bit to cut hole in lid
- semigloss paint
- wallpaper (optional)
- 4 casters
- 2 drawer pulls and bin-style drawer label

If you wish, have the home center cut the side panels, top and bottom pieces, wood strips, and the quarter-round molding.

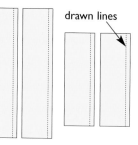

drawn lines

Working with the four side pieces, determine which side will be used for the inside of the box. Measure up from the bottom edge ¼ inch and draw a line lengthwise on each piece. This will later be used as your guide for placement of the drawer-bottom frame.

Glue and screw the side panels to the front and back panels using butt joints. The drawn lines should be on the inside of the box and should align with each other all the way around.

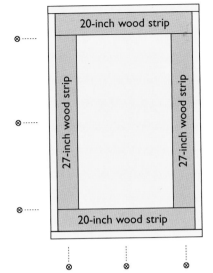

20-inch wood strip

27-inch wood strip

27-inch wood strip

20-inch wood strip

Turn the box so that the drawn lines are uppermost. Glue the narrow edge of a 20-inch wood strip to the inside front and back panels, aligning the bottom edge of each wood strip with the drawn line, creating a ¼-inch space between the bottom of the side panels and the bottom of the wood strips. Repeat to attach the 27-inch strips along the sides. The strips should fit tightly. When all wood strips have been inserted, recheck that all are aligned with the drawn lines.

Working from the outside of the box, attach the side, front, and back panels to the wood strips with 1½-inch wood screws, countersinking the screws. Use three screws on each side, centering the first and spacing the remaining two screws an equal distance on either side.

Turn the box over. Set one of the 20×30-inch pieces of plywood in the bottom of the box on top of the frame. Secure it with ¾-inch nails. Do not glue.

In each corner, glue and nail a length of quarter-round molding,

resting one end on the box bottom. There should be a ¼-inch space between the top of the quarter-round molding and the top of the box. Glue wood buttons over the countersunk screws along the sides of the box.

For the lid, find and lightly mark the center on the remaining 20×30-inch piece of plywood. Using a paddle bit, drill a hole at the mark.

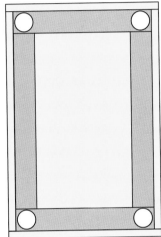

Sand the box and lid if desired; then paint the entire box and lid. Line the bottom of the box with wallpaper if desired.

Attach casters to the bottom of the box in each corner of the wood-strip frame.

Attach drawer pulls and drawer label to the front (narrow end) of the box.

167

Pear-Stamped Towel
Designed by Joe Boehm

Materials
- dish towel
- pear (or other fruit)
- star stamp or star-shape sponge
- acrylic fabric paint and textile medium
- paper towels
- disposable paper plate

Wash and dry the towel; do not use fabric softener.

Cut the pear in half. For the star design, use a star stamp or a star-shape sponge.

Pour acrylic fabric paint onto a disposable plate and mix in textile medium according to the manufacturer's instructions. Press the pear into the paint, blot the excess on a paper towel, and then press the fruit half onto the dish towel. Repeat the procedure to apply the stars.

Let the paint dry according to the manufacturer's instructions. To set, press from the wrong side with an iron on low heat.

170

Love Note Clip
Designed by Barb Vaske

Materials
- alligator clip from hardware store (found with electrical supplies)
- lead-free silver solder (found with the plumbing supplies at a hardware store)
- wire cutters
- pliers and needlenose pliers

Cut a 6-inch length of silver solder, using the wire cutters. Insert one end of the solder into the alligator clip and squeeze the base of the clip tightly around the solder, using pliers.

Grasp the free end of the solder with the needlenose pliers and twist the solder into a spiral.

Insert the free end into a piece of fruit and add your note. The fruit should last as a note-holder for at least several days. Discard the fruit when it becomes overripe.

132

Hallway Gallery
Designed by Carrie Hansen

Materials
- photos of similar size
- frames with mats 3 to 4 inches larger all around than the photos
- paint to match wall color
- laser printouts of quotation
- crafts knife
- double-stick tape
- white paint marker

Use black and white photos that are similar in composition (all "head shots," for example) for the best effect.

Use matching frames, and paint the mats to match the wall color.

The quotation that runs along the chair rail under the gallery of photos reads, "The quality of life is determined by the people in it."

To create the stencil letters for the quote, use a computer to print out the words, enlarging the letters to the desired size. (It will take several sheets of paper.) Tape all the pages together to create a scroll bearing the quote. With a crafts knife, cut out the letters. Adhere the scroll to the wall with double-stick tape. (If you have a chair rail, you can rest the bottom edge of the paper on the rail to make sure the quote is straight on the wall.)

Trace each letter with a white paint marker. To add "counterspaces" in letters such as "q," "a," and "o," align the letter itself with the outline just drawn and trace the center shape.

Remove the paper from the wall and fill in the letters with the paint marker, going over each one several times if necessary.

154

155

Cranberry Cheesecake Shake

Makes: four 8-ounce servings

Ingredients
- 1 3-ounce package cream cheese, softened
- 1 cup milk
- 2 cups vanilla ice cream
- ½ of a 16-ounce can jellied cranberry sauce
- 1 cup fresh cranberries
- Sugared cranberries (optional)*

Place cream cheese and milk in a blender container. Cover and blend until combined. Add ice cream, cranberry sauce, and the 1 cup cranberries. Cover and blend until nearly smooth, stopping to scrape down sides if necessary. Serve immediately. If desired, garnish with sugared cranberries.

*Note: For sugared cranberries, freeze whole fresh cranberries; roll in sugar until coated.

Nutrition Facts per serving: 385 cal., 21 g total fat (13 g sat. fat), 73 mg chol., 163 mg sodium, 45 g carbo., 2 g fiber, 6 g pro. Daily Values: 25% vit. A, 8% vit. C, 18% calcium, 2% iron

Strawberry Gelato

Makes: about fourteen ½-cup servings

Ingredients
- 2 cups reduced-fat milk
- 1 cup refrigerated or frozen egg product, thawed
- ½ cup sugar
- 4 cups strawberries
- 1 teaspoon lemon juice
- Fresh strawberries (optional)
- Fresh oregano (optional)

In a medium saucepan combine milk, egg product, and sugar. Cook and stir over medium heat about 10 minutes or until mixture is thickened. Do not boil. Remove saucepan from heat.

Place saucepan in a sink or bowl of ice water for 1 to 2 minutes, stirring constantly. Pour custard mixture into a bowl; set aside.

Place strawberries in a blender container or food processor bowl. Cover and blend or process until nearly smooth. Stir the strawberries and lemon juice into the custard mixture. Cover the surface of custard with plastic wrap. Refrigerate for several hours or overnight until completely chilled. (Or to chill quickly, place bowl in a sink of ice water.)

Freeze mixture in a 2- or 3-quart ice cream freezer according to the manufacturer's directions. If desired, serve with additional fresh strawberries and garnish with oregano.

Nutrition Facts per serving: 65 cal., 1 g total fat (0 g sat. fat), 3 mg chol., 41 mg sodium, 12 g carbo., 1 g fiber, 3 g pro. Daily Values: 41% vit. C Exchanges: ½ Fruit, ½ Milk

156

Greek-Style Shrimp Salad

Makes: 4 servings

Ingredients
- 1 pound fresh or frozen large shrimp in shells
- 1 recipe Lemon-Oregano Vinaigrette
- 4 cups torn mixed salad greens
- 1 medium cucumber, quartered lengthwise and cut into ¼-inch slices
- 1 medium tomato, cut into thin wedges
- ¼ cup chopped red onion
- ¼ cup thinly sliced radishes
- ¼ cup crumbled feta cheese (1 ounce)

Thaw shrimp, if frozen. Peel and devein shrimp, leaving tails intact. Rinse shrimp; pat dry. In a small bowl combine shrimp and half of the Lemon-Oregano Vinaigrette. Cover and marinate at room temperature for 30 minutes. Cover; chill remaining Lemon-Oregano Vinaigrette.

Meanwhile, in a large bowl combine greens, cucumber, tomato, onion, and radishes; toss to combine. Set aside.

Drain shrimp, reserving marinade. Thread shrimp onto eight 8-inch metal skewers, leaving ¼ inch between pieces. Grill on the greased rack of an uncovered grill directly over medium coals for 6 to 8 minutes or until shrimp are opaque, turning and brushing once with reserved marinade. Discard any remaining marinade.

To serve, divide greens mixture among 4 dinner plates. Sprinkle with feta cheese. Top each salad with 2 skewers of grilled shrimp. Serve with remaining Lemon-Oregano Vinaigrette.

Lemon-Oregano Vinaigrette: In a small bowl stir together 2 tablespoons powdered fruit pectin; 2 teaspoons snipped fresh oregano or ½ teaspoon dried oregano, crushed; 1 teaspoon sugar; ⅛ teaspoon pepper; and dash salt. Stir in ⅓ cup water; 3 tablespoons lemon juice; 3 tablespoons white wine vinegar; 1 teaspoon Dijon-style mustard; and 1 small clove garlic, minced. Cover and refrigerate for up to 3 days. Makes about ⅔ cup.

Nutrition Facts per serving: 138 cal., 3 g total fat (1 g sat. fat), 136 mg chol., 331 mg sodium, 13 g carbo., 2 g fiber, 17 g pro. Daily Values: 46% vit. C, 23% iron Exchanges: 2½ Vegetable, 1½ Meat

Warm Fajita Salad
Makes: 4 servings

Ingredients
- ¼ cup lime juice
- ¼ cup reduced-sodium chicken broth
- 1 tablespoon snipped fresh cilantro
- 2 cloves garlic, minced
- 1½ teaspoons cornstarch
- 12 ounces boneless beef top sirloin steak, cut into thin bite-size strips
- ½ teaspoon ground cumin
- ¼ teaspoon salt
- ¼ teaspoon black pepper
- Nonstick cooking spray
- 2 small onions, cut into thin wedges
- 1 medium green, red, and/or yellow sweet pepper, cut into thin strips
- 1 tablespoon cooking oil
- 1 10-ounce package torn mixed salad greens (8 cups)
- 12 cherry tomatoes and/or yellow pear tomatoes, quartered
- 1 recipe Baked Tortilla Wedges (optional)
- Salsa (optional)

In a small bowl combine lime juice, chicken broth, cilantro, garlic, and cornstarch; set aside.

In a small bowl sprinkle beef with cumin, salt, and pepper; toss to coat. Lightly coat a cold wok or large skillet with nonstick cooking spray. Preheat over medium heat. Stir-fry onion and sweet pepper for 3 to 4 minutes or until crisp-tender. Remove vegetables from wok.

Carefully add oil to wok. Add beef strips; stir-fry about 3 minutes or to desired doneness. Push to the sides of the skillet. Stir lime juice mixture; add to skillet. Cook and stir until thickened and bubbly. Cook and stir for 1 minute more. Stir meat and vegetables into sauce mixture; heat through.

To serve, arrange salad greens and tomatoes on 4 serving plates. Divide beef-vegetable mixture among plates. If desired, top with Baked Tortilla Wedges and serve with salsa.

Nutrition Facts per serving: 242 cal., 12 g total fat (4 g sat. fat), 57 mg chol., 235 mg sodium, 13 g carbo., 3 g fiber, 22 g pro. Daily Values: 100% vit. C, 24% iron Exchanges: 2½ Vegetable, 2½ Meat, 1 Fat

Baked Tortilla Wedges:
Cut 2 flour or corn tortillas into 8 wedges. Place wedges on a baking sheet. Lightly coat with nonstick cooking spray. Bake in a 400° oven for 5 minutes. Turn and bake for 3 to 5 minutes more.

Pasta with Ricotta and Vegetables
Makes: 4 servings

Ingredients
- 8 ounces dried penne or ziti
- 2½ cups fresh broccoli flowerets
- 1½ cups 1-inch pieces fresh asparagus or green beans
- 2 large ripe tomatoes
- 1 cup light ricotta cheese
- ¼ cup shredded fresh basil
- 4 teaspoons snipped fresh thyme
- 4 teaspoons balsamic vinegar
- 1 tablespoon olive oil
- 1 clove garlic, minced
- ½ teaspoon salt
- ½ teaspoon freshly ground black pepper
- 2 tablespoons grated Parmesan or Romano cheese
- Fresh thyme (optional)

Cook pasta according to package directions, adding broccoli and asparagus or beans during the last 3 minutes of cooking.

Meanwhile, place a fine strainer over a large bowl. Cut tomatoes in half; squeeze seeds and juice into strainer. With the back of a spoon, press seeds to extract juice; discard seeds. Add ricotta cheese, basil, thyme, vinegar, oil, garlic, salt, and pepper to tomato juice; mix well. Chop tomatoes; stir into ricotta mixture.

Drain pasta and vegetables; add to bowl and toss well. Sprinkle with Parmesan or Romano cheese. If desired, garnish with thyme.

Nutrition Facts per serving: 368 cal., 8 g total fat (1 g sat. fat), 12 mg chol., 393 mg sodium, 57 g carbo., 6 g fiber, 19 g pro. Daily Values: 140% vit. C, 14% calcium, 26% iron Exchanges: ½ Vegetable, 3 Starch, 1 Meat, ½ Fat

Cherry Puff
Makes: 6 servings

Ingredients
- 1 16-ounce can pitted tart red cherries (water pack)
- ½ cup sugar
- 2 tablespoons quick-cooking tapioca
- 2 egg whites
- ¼ teaspoon cream of tartar
- ⅛ teaspoon salt
- 2 egg yolks
- ⅓ cup sugar
- ⅓ cup all-purpose flour

Drain cherries, reserving ½ cup liquid. Transfer cherries to a medium saucepan. Add reserved cherry liquid, the ½ cup sugar, and the tapioca. Cook and stir over medium heat until mixture boils; reduce heat. Simmer, uncovered, for 5 minutes, stirring constantly; keep warm.

In a medium mixing bowl beat egg whites, cream of tartar, and salt with an electric mixer on medium speed until stiff peaks form (tips stand straight); set aside. In a small mixing bowl beat egg yolks for 2 to 3 minutes or until thick and lemon-colored; add the ⅓ cup sugar. Beat 1 minute more. Stir a small amount of egg white mixture into egg yolk mixture to lighten. Fold remaining egg yolk mixture into egg white mixture. Sprinkle flour over egg mixture; fold in.

Pour hot cherry mixture into a 1½-quart casserole or into six 6- to 8-ounce casseroles or custard cups. Pour batter over cherry mixture. Bake in a 325° oven for 35 to 40 minutes for the 1½-quart casserole or about 30 minutes for the small casseroles or custard cups or until top springs back when lightly touched. Serve warm.

Nutrition Facts per serving: 216 cal., 2 g total fat (1 g sat. fat), 71 mg chol., 72 mg sodium, 48 g carbo., 1 g fiber, 3 g pro. Daily Values: 4% vit. A, 5% vit. C, 2% calcium, 4% iron

Rhubarb-Raspberry-Apple Pie
Makes: 8 servings

Ingredients
- 1 recipe Pastry for Double-Crust Pie
- 1¼ cups sugar
- 3 tablespoons cornstarch
- 2 tablespoons all-purpose flour
- 4 cups chopped fresh rhubarb or frozen rhubarb
- 2 cups fresh raspberries
- 1 medium cooking apple, peeled and shredded (about ¾ cup)
- 1 to 2 tablespoons milk
- 2 to 3 teaspoons sugar (optional)

Prepare Pastry for Double-Crust Pie. On a lightly floured surface, roll half of the pastry into a 12-inch circle. Line a 9-inch pie plate with pastry. Trim pastry ½ inch beyond edge of pie plate. Fold under extra pastry. Line pastry with double thickness of foil. Bake in a 450° oven for 8 minutes. Remove foil. Bake for 5 to 6 minutes more or until golden brown. Cool on a wire rack. On a lightly floured surface, roll remaining pastry into a 12-inch circle. Using a 2- to 3-inch cutter, cut pastry into desired shapes. Cover cutouts loosely; set aside.

Meanwhile, in a large saucepan stir together the sugar, cornstarch, and flour. Stir in rhubarb, raspberries, and apple. Cook over low heat, stirring frequently, until fruit begins to juice out. Increase heat to medium. Cook and stir over medium heat until thickened and bubbly. Transfer to the baked pie shell. Brush edge of pie with milk. Place pastry cutouts over fruit filling and around the edge of the pie. Brush pastry cutouts with milk and, if desired, sprinkle with sugar. Bake in a 375° oven about 25 minutes or until pastry is golden brown. Cool on a wire rack.

Nutrition Facts per serving: 429 cal., 18 g total fat (4 g sat. fat), 0 mg chol., 138 mg sodium, 65 g carbo., 5 g fiber, 4 g pro. Daily Values: 1% vit. A, 23% vit. C, 7% calcium, 10% iron

Pastry for Double-Crust Pie: For a conventional pie with a filling that doesn't require precooking, line pie plate with half of the pastry, as directed above, except do not trim pastry or fold under. Omit the prebaking step. Set pie plate aside. To prepare filling, omit the cornstarch and reduce the raspberries to 1 cup. In a large mixing bowl stir together the sugar and, if using fresh rhubarb, 6 tablespoons of all-purpose flour. (If using frozen rhubarb, increase the all-purpose flour to ½ cup.) Stir in the rhubarb, raspberries, and apple. Transfer filling to the pastry-lined plate. Trim pastry even with rim of pie plate. Cut slits in top crust; place crust over filling. Seal; flute edge. Cover edges with foil. Bake in a 375° oven for 25 minutes. Remove foil; bake 20 to 25 minutes more or until top is golden and fruit is tender. Cool on a wire rack.

Bringing Comfort Home

*light...*For **WINDOW TREATMENTS** that soften the architecture and filter light without blocking it, check **Pottery Barn's** embroidered sheer organdy or nubby linen draperies. For a catalog, call **800/922-5507,** or visit the website at **potterybarn.com. Restoration Hardware** is another accessible source, featuring sheer, opaque, and subtly textured Belgian linen draperies, as well as breezy silk organzas. Call **800/762-1005** for a catalog or visit the website at **restorationhardware.com.** Armchair travelers seeking soft window treatments with more ethnic flair will enjoy the selection at **Anthropologie,** with sheer drapery designs ranging from kimono-inspired silk embroideries to hippy-chic florals and patchworks of silk and lace. Visit **anthropologie.com** or call **800/543-1039** for a catalog.

THEATRICAL SCRIM, a gauzy lightweight fabric, is available at some fabric stores and home decorating shops. Also check online at **rosebrand.com** Order **cable rods and curtain clips** from **Smith & Noble Windowware**; call **800/248-8888** for a catalog.

FRAMED PHOTOS shown on page 13 are by Toni Herman. For information, call **Panaché, 630/587-1090.**

Natural light is optimal, but those who depend on artificial light in their homes can take comfort in today's range of **INTERIOR LIGHTING OPTIONS** which, when thoughtfully varied, can approximate the day's changing lights. Incandescent tungsten bulbs emit a yellowish light and are best used during the morning hours in bedrooms, baths, and breakfast nooks, where they evoke the uneven, golden glow of a southern exposure. Full-spectrum bulbs are the closest replication of natural light available, emitting the same balance of colors as overhead sunlight while reducing glare and eyestrain. Useful as task lighting replacing the murky dull white of overhead lighting in kitchens, dressing rooms, or home offices, full-spectrum bulbs are also available in the form of light boxes. These portable boxes are used to alleviate symptoms associated with the winter doldrums (seasonal affective disorder), jet lag, fatigue, and insomnia. Halogen lights are also good for capturing true color, replicating the even, white illumination of a northern exposure. Use low-voltage halogen lighting to illuminate art, or install halogen bulbs in a crafts room or studio. At night, choose shaded lamps, uplights such as sconces and chandeliers, or moody wall washers instead of harsh overhead lighting. Avoid traditional fluorescent lighting, which can increase irritability and fatigue. For more information on **DESIGNING A HOUSEHOLD LIGHTING PLAN,** and for links to retail showrooms, visit the Consumer Resources page of the website of the **American Lighting Association** at **americanlightingassoc.com.**

Sculpt space and create inviting ambience with light using **DIMMER SWITCHES.** If you don't want to bother with replacing wall switches with dimmers, use lamp dimmers. Simply plug a table lamp into the dimmer and plug the dimmer cord into the wall. Dimmers save electricity and extend bulb life, too. Look for them at home improvement centers and lighting stores.

For **REMOTE-CONTROL LIGHTING** that covers your whole house, look into **Lutron's RadioRa** whole-house lighting control system. It uses a regulated radio frequency that isn't affected by power lines, cordless phones, or other wireless products and gives you one-touch control of any light or group of lights in the house. Installing the system involves replacing standard light switches with RadioRA dimmers and switches and plugging lamps into table lamp controls. Installation and setup must be done by an electrician, who also can link the controls to your home security system and a RadioRa car visor control that lets you turn lights on and off from the car. The cost of installation averages $200 to $300 per location in your home—so equipping the entry and the master bedroom, for example, would run between $400 and $600. For more information, visit the website at **lutron.com/radiora** or call the Lutron Hotline, **800/523-9466.**

For **LAMPSHADES** that make a creative decorative statement, check out boutiques such as **Panaché** in St. Charles, Illinois. Owner Cheryl Herman also refurbishes vintage lamps and adds stylish shades covered with beads, embroidered silk, or patchwork. Visit Panachè at 210 Cedar Avenue; call **630/587-1090** for information. (Travelers will also enjoy browsing her collection of imported bath and body products and unique home decorating accessories.)

For unusual, well-made **CANDLES,** from votives and pillars to tea lights and tapers, as well as attractive containers and candleholders, check out **Illuminations.com.** The company has a catalog and retail outlets as well. The candlemakers at **Ephemera** approach candlemaking like sculpture. Retailers from **Henri Bendel** and the **Terence Conran Shop** in New York to **Harrods** in London carry these affordable examples of candle-making art in evocative, modernist shapes and a warm, natural palette of ivories, butter yellows, sable greens, and moss grays. For more information, visit **ephemera.com.**

For **CANDLE SAFETY,** never leave a burning candle unattended and keep wicks trimmed to ⅛ to ¼ inch. If the tip of a wick has curled to one side, it has burned too long. To approximate the burning time of a quality candle, multiply one hour per each inch of candle diameter. Candles kept in one place for a long period of time should be rotated occasionally to allow for even burning. Never let matches burn in the candle's pool of melting wax; watch for drips from drafts, and keep burning candles away from enclosed spaces like bookshelves. Extinguish candles that have burned down to within 2 inches of their holders.

For sconces, chandeliers, or candleholders placed on fine furniture, use **DRIPLESS CANDLES.** Or add a **BOBECHE** to your candleholder to catch dripping wax. Most bobeches fit standard taper holders and are available in a variety of materials. **The Bombay Company** offers dressy yet economical decorative bobeches made of a sturdy clear plastic with hanging prisms and beads for extra sparkle. Visit **bombayco.com** to shop online or locate a store near you or call **800/829-7789** for a catalog. Natural **BEESWAX CANDLES** add texture to a table and, unlike many less expensive candles made from petroleum products, have a high melting point that can make them nearly dripless and smokeless.

As an **ALTERNATIVE TO CANDLES,** try **CANDELAS,** cone-shape tabletop lamps that run on rechargeable batteries and glow like candles without the safety issues of dripping wax or unattended flames. Look for them at **vesselinc.com.**

fragrance...**DRIED LAVENDER** stems are sold in packages at crafts stores. To buy lavender buds in bulk, check local health food stores, or order online. **Tom Thumb Workshops,** 59 Market St., Onancock, Virginia, sells dried lavender stems as well as essential oils; call **800/526-6502** or visit the website at **tomthumbworkshops.com.** To order lavender buds direct from Provence, try **provence-scents.com. Jardin du Soleil Lavender Farm** in Sequim, Washington, sells lavender buds in bulk, along with aromatherapy and herbal products, linen water, soaps, and gifts. Visit the website at **jardindusoleil.com** or call **877/527-3461.**

L'Occitane en Provence is a splendid source of herbal- and floral-based **FRAGRANCES** for the home and body, offering products for both men and women. Editor's personal favorites: Vetiver and Tilleul eau de toilettes and solid amber home fragrance. Call **888/623-2880** for store locations, or visit the website at **loccitane.com.**

SCENTED CANDLES are widely available at discount stores and superstores, but know that when it comes to quality, you get what you pay for. Many inexpensive, chemically-scented candles can burn dirty and emit toxins into the air. Handmade candles are best, scented with essential oils and made from a food-grade paraffin wax. For the best scents, check out shops that specialize in home fragrances, aromatherapy products, and bath fragrances. **Illuminations** at **illuminations.com** offers a good selection. One of the best gardenia-scented candles comes from **Illume Candles Inc.** The fragrance is absolutely true and scents the room even without being lit. Visit the website at **illumecandles.com** to see their product line; orders can be placed by phone. Call **800/245-5863** between 10 a.m. and 6 p.m. PST.

AROMATHERAPY FOR KIDS is available in baby products from **Johnson** and toys by **SmartScents, Fisher-Price,** and **Hasbro;** look for the toys at specialty stores and mass merchants such as **JC Penney** and **Toys "R" Us.** Research indicates that scent can enhance learning ability in infants by stimulating a part of the brain that is normally inactive.

A wonderfully fragrant alternative to the usual packaged potpourris is **Cote Bastide AMBER CRYSTALS Potpourri.** The rocklike chunks are saturated with a rich, spicy, vanilla-based scent. When the fragrance fades, reawaken it with the refresher oil. Look for it at boutiques and specialty shops or order online from **Beautydoor, dots2com.**

Kiel's, an apothecary since 1851, has intoxicated New Yorkers for more than 150 years with the clean, warm, earthy scent of their original Musk Oil. They also offer a variety of new essences (Chinese flowers, cucumber, grapefruit, patchouli, and coriander) as well as bath specialty products. Gift sets of Kiehl's products are packaged in a classic white box, nestled in a bed of potpourri in themes to suit "the jet-setter" or "baby's gentle care." Kiehl's flagship store at 109 Third Avenue between 13th and 14th Streets, NYC 10003, **212/677-3171** and a second location at 2360 Filmore Street in San Francisco, **415/359-9260** are visual treats to visit, with staff dressed in white coats as in an old apothecary. Outside of these cities, visit the website at **kiehls.com** for a list of products and national retailers (including **Barneys, Neiman Marcus** and **Saks Fifth Avenue**); or call **800/KIEHLS2 (800/543-4572)** to shop by phone.

For more **AVANT-GARDE TRENDS IN FRAGRANCE,** try the hand-blended scents of **Demeter.** Each fragrance is unusual yet familiar, using only natural essential oils to conjure up favorite foods ("brownie," "tiramisu," or "crème brûlée"), times or places ("birthday cake" or "laundromat"), and the changing seasons. Winter scents include "snow," "fireplace," or "fruit cake," while summery fragrances like "dirt," "grass," and "tomato" (smells just like ripening vines) allow urban dwellers to indulge their inner gardener. Available through **Sephora** stores, **sephora.com** or hip, local retailers such as **Whatever,** a home accessories store voted "Des Moines's Best Place to Indulge your Inner Child" at 855 42nd Street, Des Moines, IA 50312, **515/255-1739.**

sound...
For an **ANTIQUE MILLSTONE** to make a fountain, check architectural salvage companies. Another possible source for manufactured or antique millstones is **Anne Hathaway Cabin and Cottage Antiques,** Tula at Bennet Street, Atlanta, GA 30309; **404/352-4153.**

Smith & Hawken offers pleasant-sounding wind chimes and elegant stone and copper birdbaths to attract the songs of feathered friends, as well as a timpani fountain that combines the chimes of floating brass bells with the gentle rush of flowing water. Visit **smith-hawken.com** or call **800/940-1170** for a catalog.

To reduce background office noise or the clatter of outside traffic, try nestling down with a good book wearing a **Bose Noise-Cancelling** headset. The full-spectrum noise reduction system was originally designed for pilots and features soft ear cushions for extended wear and is available through **Hammacher Schlemmer** (**hammacherschlemmer.com**). Or counter distracting noises with sounds of your own. **HoMedics,** sold through department stores, makes a tiny, portable and very economical "**SoundSpa Acoustic Relaxation**" machine with six recorded sounds, including ocean waves and spring rain.

the bed...
The **SOFTEST SHEETS** on the market today are made from 100% Egyptian cotton or American pima cotton (labeled with the trademark "Supima"). Knowing the type of cotton is often a better indicator of quality than thread count. For beautiful bedding to buy online or by catalog, some of the best-known companies are **Garnet Hill** (**garnethill.com**), **The Company Store** (**thecompanystore.com**), and **Land's End** (**landsend.com**). Land's End sells oxford-cloth sheets that feel like your favorite shirt; also shop here for spa-style waffle-weave towels, luxuriously soft fleece throws, and furniture. **Chambers** sells exquisite high-end imported bedding, towels, lavender linen water, some furniture and accessories, and sleepwear. Call **800/334-9790** for a catalog. Shopping pros recommend watching for their sales.

ABC Carpet & Home in New York City (**212/473-3000**) and Delray Beach, FL (**561/279-7777**), well-known for quality handwoven Oriental carpets, is also a large retailer of extra-luxury bedding including soft wool and cashmere blankets, fluffy down pillows and comforters, natural cotton matelassé coverlets, regal Italian damask sheets, and silk charmeuse duvet covers. Visit online at abccarpet.com.

If you're in Washington, D.C., visit **Baldaquin** at 1413 Wisconsin Ave. NW (**202/625-1600; 800/525-4849**). Occupying an old townhouse in Georgetown, this high-end shop features **FINE LINENS, CASHMERE THROWS, PILLOWS, CUSTOM BEDS FROM FRANCE,** and more for bedroom and bath, displayed in intimate and inviting room settings. Dining rooms showcase **FINE SILVER, CRYSTAL, AND CHINA**. It's worth a visit for decorating ideas as well as gifts for yourself and others; or visit on the web at **baldaquin.com**.

For **VINTAGE LINENS,** check estate sales, antiques shops, and antiques fairs, as well as online auctions such as **ebay** and **Yahoo Auctions.**

There's nothing like feeling hip while feeling toasty warm. **Fashy** (short for "Fashion Hot"), a German thermoplastics accessory manufacturer, have made your **GRANDMOM'S HOT WATER BOTTLE** a must-have winter accessory. Available in too-cute shapes such as a plastic perfume bottle with floating red hearts, a giant red heart, or in the form of a plush, cuddly teddy bear (the hot water bottle zips inside). Sold in drugstores and department stores or through **drugstore.com.**

The **ELECTRIC FIREPLACE** with mantel shown on page 60 is manufactured by **Dimplex.** To view the full line of mantels and grills, visit the website at **dimplex.com. Heat-N-Glo,** a division of **Hearth Technologies,** also makes electric fireplaces. Visit their website at **heatnglo.com.**

For a selection of antique monogrammed **EUROPEAN BEDSHEETS,** as well as quality antique kitchen and table linens, try the online "Linen Room" of Connecticut dealer **Cynthia Cooper** (**antique-linens.com**). For a new set of bedsheets personalized with your own initials, shop at retailers with bridal registries. Many such retailers provide monogramming services themselves, while others can recommend a local monogramming business.

If you and your bed partner have different body temperatures, try Martex **X-STATIC SHEETS**; the easy-care fabric contains silver fibers that adjust to ambient temperature. The fibers also prevent static and have anti-microbial properties. Visit **martex.com** for products and store information.

Sobagara (sobagara.com) is a quality supplier of **BUCKWHEAT HULL PILLOWS.** The stuffing, composed of the outside part of the buckwheat seed milled off before grinding, is hypoallergenic and long-lasting. It conforms to your body as you move, stimulating acupressure points while dissipating heat so you stay warm in winter and cool in summer. In addition to standard pillows, Sobarga offers baby pillows, travel pillows, eye pillows, body pillows and even pet beds.

the bath... Recommended retail shops include the Midwest's most upscale general store, **C.S. Post & Co.** of Hays, Kansas, a rich source for **PLUSH ORGANIC BATH TOWELS AND LINENS** combining functional materials with luxurious spa comfort (such as high-pile cotton terry towels lined with crisp 100% Italian linen). Other items of interest include textured hemp rugs, a selection of antique suitcases, and aromatherapeutic, plant-derived household cleansers (available as a gift set in an old-fashioned galvanized bucket). Call C.S. Post & Co. toll-free **888/419-2399** or visit **cspost.com.** Travelers with a hankering for fine bath products will also want to stop in Fredericksburg, Texas, where The **Homestead**, a shop on Main Street, sells an amazing array of **BED AND BATH PRODUCTS** and linen waters, as well as white ironstone reproduction tabletop items and unusual home furnishings and accessories. Field editor Joetta Moulden says it's worth the trip just to see how they display their wares.

VINTAGE EUROPEAN-INSPIRED ACCESSORIES from **Ballard Designs** can help complete the spa-at-home experience. Shop **ballarddesigns.com** or call **800/367-2775** for a catalog offering fleur-de-lis bath mats, scrolled iron fixtures and towel holders, powder-room-size crystal chandeliers and more.

Crabtree & Evelyn is a reputable and reliable source of **BATH AND BODY TREATS** and home fragrances, loved for their pretty scents and old-fashioned packaging. Call **800/272-2873** or visit **crabtree-evelyn.com.** For true **ANTIQUE APOTHECARY RECIPES** in historical packaging, there's **Caswell-Massey**, a manufacturer of soaps, lotions, and colognes with an American heritage dating back to 1752, when Ben Franklin is reputed to have brought the fashion for luxury bathing back from Paris. George Washington preferred their Cologne #6, while sharpshooter Annie Oakley, actress Sarah Bernhardt, and later, the Eisenhower presidency, favored herbaceous products ranging from soothing almond cream soaps and shave cream to flower waters and rose-infused face powder papers for a quick daytime "freshening up." Search **caswell-massey.com** for a list of retailers.

Camille Beckman, headquartered in Boise, Idaho, makes Glycerine Hand Therapy based on an old family recipe. The creamy lotion comes in a variety of delightful fragrances, including Oriental Spice, French Vanilla, White Lilac, and Gardenia Breeze. Also available are bath and body products, candles, room sprays and drawer sachets. To find a retail source near you, visit the website at **camillebeckman.com.**

For a change of pace from the traditional floral-scented bath, try **Philosophy**, an alternative skin care manufacturer that has quickly become the girlfriend's choice for catchy-named bath and body gift sets. Incorporating the effects of **COLOR THERAPY, AROMATHERAPY, AND PHEROMONE TECHNOLOGY,** these products soothe the body while triggering happy sensory memories including that of favorite comfort foods. Try the bright pink "Strawberry Milk Shake" shampoo or the "Cookbook—Homemade Pies" rainbow set of coconut-cream, lemon-meringue, key-lime and blueberry-pie bath and body washes. Available at **Sephora** stores (for locations, visit **sephora.com**) or through major department stores. Sephora, a growing cosmetics chain, is a hip source for a wide selection of sensory cosmetics, cutting-edge fragrances and bath products.

For an **ALL-OVER WATER MASSAGE,** check out the new showerhead from **Moen.** Its patented Revolution massaging showerhead sends out a spiral of water that can be dialed up for deep massage or down to a rainlike shower. It's available for about $60 at **Lowe's, Target, Bed Bath and Beyond,** plumbing showrooms, and online at the company's website (see below). The fixture isn't considered low-flow, but all showerheads are limited by federal regulation to 5.5 gallons per minute (old showerheads could use as much as 8 gallons per minute) and it isn't affected by low water pressure. For more information, visit the website at **moen.com.** The Nature S Curve showerhead ($40) by **Aquatek International** drenches you with even pressure from every point on the 5½-inch-diameter head. Call **800/640-4139** or visit the website, **aquatekinternational.com.** To install these and most other showerheads onto standard water pipes, remove the old fixture and clean the pipe threads. Wrap the shower arm with Teflon for a secure seal, then screw on the new showerhead.

HEATED TOWEL RACKS can be ordered from **Warmrails, Inc., 877/927-6724; warmrails.com; Comfort House, comforthouse.com; Chambers, 800/334-9790;** and **Hammacher Schlemmer** (the source of the towel rack pictured on page 70), **800/543-3366.**

The terry-covered dressing stool pictured on page 68 is no longer available, but Chambers offers wooden **BENCHES WITH TERRY COVERED CUSHIONS.** Call **800/334-9790** for a catalog.

space...**Pottery Barn** offers affordable chenille throws, pillows, **SINK-IN SEATING**, and ottomans for your feet. For a catalog, call **800/922-5507** or visit the website at **potterybarn.com**. For **PILLOW SLIPCOVERS, QUILTS, COVERLETS, AND SHEETS** in Provençal-inspired cottons as well as velvets, corduroy, and embroidered sheers in winter and spring color themes, visit **April Cornell**, a retail chain. To find a store near you, visit the website at **aprilcornell.com**.

Especially Lace, (202 Fifth Street, West Des Moines, IA 50265) in Valley Junction, sells ANTIQUE AND NEW LACE curtains and linens as well as selected items from the April Cornell line and products from Jardin du Soleil, Crabtree & Evelyn, The Good Home, and more. Worth a visit in person or on the web at **especiallylace.com**

In Houston, West Alabama is the street to shop for **WONDERFUL STUFF. Kuhl-Linscomb,** 2424 West Alabama, offers unusual dishes, glassware, and white ironstone, raffia throw pillows, wicker and rattan, fine linens, and a lavish bed, bath, and candle selection; **713/526-6000.** At 3600 West Alabama, **Thompson + Hansen** is a nursery with a great gift shop offering crunchy coir and sea-grass rugs, Kenneth Turner candles, and overscaled accessories such as bowls, urns, and candlesticks; **713/622-6973.** Field editor Joetta Moulden likes to shop here for decorating ideas as well as accessories.

In San Francisco, visit **Sue Fisher King** at 3067 Sacramento St. for exquisite bed linens from Anichini, exclusive Italian velvet throws and pillows, dinnerware and glassware in simple but beautiful shapes and colors, table linens, and unusual decorative objects. Online: **suefisherking.com**

In Northern Virginia, **Beekeeper's Cottage** offers everything you need for **STYLISH CASUAL COMFORT**: Shabby Chic sofas, chairs, and ottomans; April Cornell linens; Tracey Porter tabletop; vintage and French tableware and textiles; and a complete spa section with soaps, lotions, and candles. Shop two locations: 43738 Hay Rd., Ashburn, VA 20147 **(703/726-9411)** or 42350 Lucketts Rd., Leesburg, VA 20176 **(703/771-9006).** Or visit on the web at **beekeeperscottage.com**.

For ideas to create outdoor rooms, visit **bhg.com/bkfreshair. For ideas on how to craft comfortable spaces indoors and out, visit bhg.com/bkhousehome.**

order...For **HOOK RACKS** that accomplish decorative storage similar to the cornice of pegs on page 109, see the **Hold Everything** catalog; call **800/421-2264** for a copy. The catalog also offers baskets and metal boxes designed for stacking on shelves in pantries or on bookcases. **Pottery Barn** also sells a row of hooks on a wood base that can be mounted on the wall. **IKEA, Ikea-usa.com,** has just about

everything for the home at affordable prices. It's also the largest rug retailer in the world. **Pier 1 Imports** (visit **pier1.com** for a store locator) is a reliable source for **WOVEN BASKETS** in a variety of fibers, ethnic designs, and sizes ranging from laundry hampers to bread baskets and desk accessories.

Search online auctions for **ANTIQUE WALLPAPERED BANDBOXES,** or try a not-so-musty alternative. Useful for storing anything from dressing accessories to home office supplies and treasured keepsakes, the carefully handcrafted bandboxes of **Hannah's Treasures** in Harlan, Iowa, are covered with authentic vintage wallpaper (patterns date from circa 1890-1948) and lined with old newspaper print. Visit the website at **hannahstreasures.com** or call **712/755-3173.**

If you're serious about GETTING ORGANIZED and decluttering your life, visit **bhg.com/bkorganize** for lots of tips and practical ideas.

focal points...**PICTURE FRAMES** like those shown on pages 132–133 can be ordered from **Pottery Barn** (**potterybarn.com**, or call **888/779-4044** for a catalog). Original oil paintings on page 144 by Vicki Ingham; original cow painting on page 145 by Kathryn Colvig.

To start your own collection of **JAPANESE CAST-IRON TEAPOTS** (or to sample a wide selection of quality teas and herbal infusions), check out **Teavana** with five stores in Atlanta and another at the Mall of America in Bloomington, Minnesota. Visit online at **teavana.com.**

table top...For **FUN, OFFBEAT, HIP TABLEWARE AND ACCESSORIES** (and other stuff), check out **Chiasso** (Italian for "uproar"). Call **800/654-3570** or order online at **chiasso.com. Crate and Barrel** defines TRADITIONAL STYLE for the second millennium. Call **800/323-5461** for a catalog or visit online **crateandbarrel.com.**

If you're in New York City, visit **Fish Eddy's,** diagonally across from ABC Carpet & Home at 19th and Broadway. **VINTAGE AND REPRODUCTION DISHES,** platters, bowls, creamers, glassware, and mugs, as well as new designs from artists. A good place to look for old hotel dishes.

BREAKFAST IN BED is especially pampering when served on an elegant bed tray. **The Ronel Bed Tray Company** crafts fine wooden bed trays in satin white paint or a natural clear finish with adjustable tilt tables for reading and a separate tray, with handles, designed to fit onto the bed tray. Sold at high-end boutiques or available through their factory online at **breakfasttray.com.**

ACKNOWLEDGMENTS

RESEARCH Karin Baji Holms

RESOURCE ASSISTANCE Linda Krinn, Paula Marshall, Joetta Moulden

PHOTOGRAPHY JIM KRANTZ AND KRITSADA/KRANTZ STUDIOS; **STYLING** KAREN JOHNSON
pages 6, 9, 13 top left, 28, 31, 32, 33, 38, 39 top right, 41 top left, 43, 46, 50, 53, 60, 63 right, 76-77, 79, 97, 115, 125, 151, 170

PHOTOGRAPHY GUY HURKA PHOTOGRAPHY; **STYLING** ELAINE MARKOUTSAS
pages 13 top right, 24, 25, 26, 27, 130

PHOTOGRAPHY BILL HOLT PHOTOGRAPHY; **FIELD EDITORS** ELAINE MARKOUTSAS, ELLE ROPER, TRISH MAHARAM
pages 14, 23, 91

PHOTOGRAPHY KIM CORNELISON; **STYLING** PEGGY JOHNSTON
pages 16, 34-35, 89, 120, 166

PHOTOGRAPHY KING AU/STUDIO AU; **STYLING** MOLLIE PASHIBIN, SUNDIE RUPPERT
pages 18, 19, 22, 29, 34 left, 40, 67, 72, 73, 74, 75, 85, 102, 103 top,
106, 109, 113, 116, 117, 118 right, 126, 127, 128, 142–143, 144, 146

PHOTOGRAPHY PETER KRUMHARDT; **STYLING** SUNDIE RUPPERT
pages 99, 108 right, 122, 123, 132–133, 168,

PICTUREQUEST.COM
pages 48 and 49

PHOTOGRAPHY MARK LOHMAN PHOTOGRAPHY; **STYLING** Joe Ruggiero
page 147

Additional photography courtesy of the following Meredith publications: *Better Homes and Gardens* magazine, *Country Home* magazine, *Traditional Home* magazine, *Better Homes and Gardens* Do It Yourself magazine, *Better Homes and Gardens* Bedroom & Bath magazine, *Better Homes and Gardens* Garden, Deck & Landscape magazine, *Better Homes and Gardens* Decorating magazine, *Better Homes and Gardens* Home Ideas magazine, *Traditional Home Renovation Style* magazine, *Traditional Home* Decorator Showhouse magazine, *Better Homes and Gardens* The Smart Diet, and *Better Homes and Gardens* Treasured Recipes.

Special thanks to **Seasonal Concepts**, Des Moines, Iowa, for providing the electric fireplace on page 60 for photography.